KANSAS TYCOON
EMERSON CAREY

· *Building an Empire from Coal, Ice and Salt* ·

LYNN LEDEBOER AND MYRON MARCOTTE

Foreword by Michael Carey, great-grandson of Emerson Carey

THE
History
PRESS

Published by The History Press
Charleston, SC
www.historypress.com

First published 2019

Manufactured in the United States

ISBN 9781467140799

Library of Congress Control Number: 2018966329

CONTENTS

FOREWORD

When Lynn and Myron asked if I would like to write a foreword to this book, my first thought was, "OK, I haven't written anything more than a few pages since college." But here goes. I tried to think of a catchy sobriquet to start out with, and I came up with "A Man in Full." I didn't make that up; it's the name of a novel by the late author Tom Wolfe. The protagonist, an aging real estate tycoon, doesn't have much in common with Emerson, but I think the phrase does fit him.

The following pages detail Emerson's rise from very humble circumstances on a farm in Indiana to a very successful industrialist in Hutchinson, Kansas. He is not unique in that regard, of course. America has countless rags-to-riches tales from that time. Let me start out by noting the truly impressive level of scholarly research that Lynn and Myron put into this book. Although I knew quite a few of the details of Emerson's commercial ventures, this endeavor takes the facts and figures of commerce and weaves them into a story. It illustrates how these ventures began and evolved, with all the twists and turns that came about in the rough-and-tumble world of early twentieth-century industrialism. Emerson was a truly gifted individual with an enormous drive to succeed and a profound genius for making that happen. I still have trouble understanding how, with such a limited education, he could handwrite those early Conn & Carey income statements and balance sheets like a seasoned accountant in such beautiful handwriting.

I grew up hearing and knowing about Emerson and his business accomplishments, of course. My father, Jake, would take us down into the mine now and then, and we'd tour the evaporating plant, where all I wanted to see were the train cars. I knew this was all created by my great-grandfather and was properly awed.

The Emerson that I "knew," though, was not just the successful businessman. He was the romantic who created Willowbrook, where I grew up. As a free-range kid, I knew every inch of that place, and I came to understand him as I grew up. Yes, the golf course is and was the main feature of Willowbrook, and his house dominated the landscape, of course. It was always called the "White House" and was a constant reminder of Emerson. However, I was always aware of the less obvious echoes that Emerson left there. He took frequent trips to Europe, and I think he came back with ideas for classical landscaping plans, along with some marble statues from Italy. The Willowbrook landscaping plan was going to be something to rival the grand European gardens, I believe. I imagine, though, that the Great Depression and Emerson's illness in the early '30s curtailed the undertaking. Some of it lingered. I could still see traces of these designs around the pool during my childhood with its formal English layout with stone benches and shrub-lined walkways. My father said that there was once a landscaped walkway between Emerson's house and his son Howard's house. I looked and could just make out the traces of the path where a few spirea bushes still remained.

Emerson was truly a family man and a social man. I have his Willowbrook guest book, wherein every visitor wrote his or her name when they came for a function. And there were many. The first entry is Christmas Day 1921, and the third name is Laura Reed Yaggy (renowned Hutchinson violinist and advocate for women's rights), followed by the note "With a hearty welcome to our new neighbor." The largest gathering was the "Carey Family Reunion" of September 4, 1923, for which there were exactly fifty signatures, including eight of Emerson's sisters. It also has the scrawled signature of my father, Jake, who was six! All throughout the guest book, one can spot the well-known names of early Hutchinson: Colladay, Bigger, Mammel, Yaggy, McCandless, Stamey, Pegues, McNaughten, Adela Hale, Winchester, Meyer, Gano, Hipple, Gowans, Brownlee, Conklin and Whiteside.

Lynn and Myron note the institutional legacies that Emerson left. For me, those legacies also endure, and they are based on the way Emerson raised his sons and how they, in turn, passed on the traditions of philanthropy, community engagement and love of family.

I think Emerson's whole outlook on business, family and life in general is best summed up in a letter he wrote to sons Howard and Charles while they were at Cornell. It is dated January 22, 1913, and written on Kansas senate chamber letterhead.

Along with some admonishments for them to "live correct upright lives always make our word good and keep everlastingly at it," he writes:

> *I am glad we have been situated so we could spend so much time together and that we have always been so congenial. And I look forward to the many years that I hope we may all live and plan and work together for the advancement of all our interests, business, social and fraternal. If we keep our health and do teamwork as I know we shall there is nothing that this Carey family cannot accomplish. I am laying this foundation for this future which is broad enough for all of the Carey boys and their father to work on and it will be a great pleasure and satisfaction to see our plans work out. With lots and lots of love, Papa.*

A Man in Full.

—Mike Carey
Mike Carey is Emerson Carey's great-grandson.

ACKNOWLEDGEMENTS

When we started on this endeavor, we never dreamed it would take us nine months to write this book. We discovered there was a lot written about Emerson Carey; however, many of these were short biographies that only touched on specific industries or the beginning of his life. It didn't appear that there were any comprehensive books or that "one" particular book covered it all. The closest that anyone had come to this was George Simpson, to whom we are greatly indebted. In 1956, Mr. Simpson wrote his very comprehensive master's thesis for the Kansas State Teachers College, titled "A Brief History of Emerson Carey's Carey Salt Company, 1901–1956." Simpson focused on the Carey Salt Company. One of the only existing copies of this that we know of is housed at the Hutchinson Public Library. The reference librarians at the Hutchinson Public Library were exceedingly helpful—and patient—keeping this copy of the book handy specifically for us. Emerson Carey himself had the foresight to begin an autobiography that remained unfinished. His detailed accounts provided much insight into his thinking and actions. We wish to thank Mike Carey, Emerson's great-grandson, for all his advice, input, suggestions, photographs and all-around encouragement and for writing our foreword. Thank you to Steve Conard and Steve Harmon for their generosity in sharing the images from their vast and wonderful collection of Hutchinson's photographic history. Also, thanks are in order to the Hutchinson Chamber of Commerce and to the Reno County Museum for sharing images from their collections. Former Reno County Historical Society executive director

ACKNOWLEDGEMENTS

Mary Grace Clements was gracious enough to enable us to complete this biography and also encouraged us greatly. And finally, we wish to thank our long-suffering spouses, who granted us endless evenings to allow us to complete this book. Thanks, Connie Marcotte and Daniel Ledeboer!

INTRODUCTION

Y ou may be asking, "Who was Emerson Carey?" That is a good question, and it took a whole book to answer it. He was a pioneering man who stuck to his principles, worked hard and found great success. Carey was a Kansas industrialist, philanthropist, state senator, shrewd businessman and accomplished golfer, but what made him a Reno County icon was his creation of the Carey Salt Company in Hutchinson, Kansas.

Our interest in Carey comes from the fact that we help operate the Reno County Museum and Strataca-Kansas Underground Salt Museum. The Salt Museum is housed underground in the very salt mine that Carey created. Writing this book has increased our knowledge of Carey's industries and the man himself. We were amazed at the sheer number of companies, industries, interests and philanthropic activities in which Emerson Carey was involved. Each one could be a book on its own. Carey had four sons who also were quite accomplished and led admirable lives; a book about each son could easily be written as well.

We chose to follow Carey's life chronologically, from birth to death. Because he was involved in so many things simultaneously throughout his life, it was extremely difficult to include all the particulars in every industry and activity. It was our goal to show just how complicated and involved Carey's life was. It is of note that although his achievements left long-lasting legacies that still thrive today, the book itself ends at his death.

So, travel back in time with us, to a cold winter day in a log cabin in Indiana at the beginning of 1863…

CHAPTER 1

FROM RAGS

1863–1882

Excitement was in the air inside a small log house for the Carey family on this January 22, 1863 winter day in Marion, Grant County, Indiana. Samuel and Nancy were about to give birth to their third child. Having conceived two daughters, Almeda and Etta, the Careys were hoping for a son. Their new baby was a son whom they christened Emerson, a name synonymous with brave and powerful.[1]

However, while Samuel and Nancy's immediate wish for a son had been fulfilled, what they never dreamed of, nor could even have hoped for, was the incredible prosperity this son would eventually reap upon them, a prosperity full of success and wealth beyond their wildest imagination.

The family grew, as Emerson was followed by siblings Susanna, Arthur and Rose.[2] At this point in the United States' history, westward expansion was on the move. The adventurous and pioneering spirit of the new settlers took hold of many rugged individuals, including Samuel. The lure of free land offered by the Homestead Act of 1862 must have been incredibly tempting for Samuel. Later in life, a grown-up Emerson remembered of his father, "Uncle Sam had a quarter section of land out here for him and he wanted to come out and get it." So, Samuel followed his dreams of self-reliance in the search for a land claim. Samuel's drive to remain independent was possibly based on his Quaker upbringing, and in 1867, he moved the family to Plainfield, Indiana. That same year, Samuel moved the family yet again to Shelby County, Illinois.[3]

The Carey family continued to grow with the birth of Emerson's sister Elizabeth. In 1871, Samuel moved his family again to Douglas County, Illinois, and the family grew once more with the addition of another sister, Emma.[4] By 1873, the family had moved to Ridgefarm, in Vermillion County, Illinois, where they stayed for five years while continuing to seek a government land claim.[5] Perhaps Samuel was unable to procure the eighteen-dollar filing fee that was required to file an application, or perhaps he was unable to fulfill the requirement of remaining on the land for the full minimum of five years due to his adventurous and pioneering spirit.

Samuel Carey, Emerson's father.
Conard-Harmon Collection.

However, Samuel never followed through on a land claim and, therefore, often farmed on rented or leased land.[6]

Emerson's great-grandson Mike Carey related that there may have been other reasons behind the Carey family's constant moving, according to family lore. Mike explained that Samuel

> had difficulty "finding himself" during much of his life....and based on the many moves he made in Indiana, Illinois and later Kansas, seemed to be unable to settle in and make a living. The grass was always greener somewhere else....My understanding from my father [Jake] is that Samuel was an alcoholic and never settled in to anything....However, by all indications, he was apparently a good father to his children. In fairness to Samuel, the Carey family unit had been on the move for several generations before Emerson's father, Samuel, came along. John Carey came to eastern Pennsylvania from England as an indentured servant in 1725. His son married a Quaker girl, and he joined the faith. The next several generations migrated to Virginia, North Carolina, Ohio and then Indiana with other Quaker families. Each generation had ten or twelve children, and the entire family groups joined other migrating Quaker families in the search for new opportunities.

Mike suggested that with families that large, it was very difficult to divide the family farmlands between all the heirs. So, the younger generations went in search of their own lands on which to settle and cultivate.[7] Whether it was

Samuel Carey's family, with Samuel in the front row on the right. *Conard-Harmon Collection.*

a need for independent pastures, an adventurous spirit or simply "spirits," Samuel kept the Carey family on the move for many years.

Emerson's sister Bertha was born in 1875, and by 1876, thirteen-year-old Emerson often helped his father Samuel with farming. By 1878, Emerson worked for others, plowing and cultivating corn, for which he received ten dollars per month. Using twenty dollars of Emerson's hard-earned wages, in 1878 Samuel hopped aboard a train to Kansas in his never-ending search for better land, a better life and a fresh start for himself and his family.[8] He first moved to Sterling, Kansas, and summoned his family to join him. Sterling had originally been named "Peace" as a nod to Quaker N.P. Ninde, an agent of the Town Company, which founded the city in 1872. Peace eventually changed its name to Sterling in 1876.[9] Perhaps the town's Quaker origins combined with family already living there drew Samuel to the town of Sterling. Emerson's mother, Nancy, traded their small place in Vermillion County for "an old team and wagon and about $30 in money, and loaded [her] children in the wagon and started for Kansas in early October 1878."[10] On the way, the family stopped at President Abraham Lincoln's grave site in Springfield, Illinois, where his grand tomb had just recently been completed in 1874. The majestic and imposing monument with its stone obelisk, bronze horses, life-sized bronze statue of Lincoln and marble interior must have been awe-inspiring to Nancy, who went out of her way to impress upon her children how great a man Lincoln was. This experience greatly affected young Emerson. He was so taken by the story of Lincoln that he vowed to always try to emulate him. This vow guided Emerson's decision-making throughout the remainder of his life.[11]

In a fitting farewell to Illinois, Eva, in 1878, was Emerson's last sibling to be born in that state. Nancy began the journey to Kansas with her large family of ten children, including the just-born baby, Eva. Emerson's memories about the family's time in Illinois reflect the destitute nature of their time there: "We were very glad to leave that country as our family had always been poor and hard up and we had undergone many hardships....I have never visited Ridgefarm or any of the other places we lived in Illinois and I have no desire or curiosity to do so."[12]

A well-known anecdote in the story of the Carey family trip to Kansas illustrates just how desperately poor the Carey family had become. During the trip, somewhere in Missouri, Nancy and her children passed a potato farmer working his crops. Low on food and supplies, Nancy Carey stopped their covered wagon and offered to trade the farmer one of her crocks for some potatoes. The farmer, upon seeing the horde of hungry children in the wagon, told Nancy Carey to keep the crock and still gave her the sack of potatoes.[13]

Emerson's remaining three siblings were all born in Kansas: Edith in 1880, Maude in 1883 and finally baby Claude in 1886, bringing the family to a total of thirteen children. Samuel attempted to meet the family by walking to Hutchinson, but he caught up with them near Nickerson with only ten cents in his pocket, while Nancy had only a nickel. Settling in Sterling, Emerson initially found work with a Mr. Keys at the edge of town for ten dollars per month. For one month's pay, he received a "half-Texas heifer" and began a cattle herd that grew to eleven head. While in Sterling, the Carey family lived in a sod house made with pieces of sod laid in a brick-like pattern that were eighteen inches long, a foot wide and about three inches thick. Emerson remembered collecting and burning buffalo chips and corn stalks in the winter for heat.[14]

During 1879, the Careys lived with an uncle, Isaac Bundy, a half mile east of Sterling. Emerson worked on a farm while Samuel worked various other jobs to raise money. Emerson described his time in Sterling: "I run the farm and raised a small crop of corn which was burned up by the hot winds, and my father worked out to help pay the expenses of our meagre living." In the fall of 1879, the family moved yet again, this time to McPherson, Kansas.[15] However, as author Harry Stewart noted, Samuel "was a man who believed that fortune awaited him just over the hill," and so he continued to search for that pot of gold, while Emerson remained in McPherson working the farm.[16]

Sometime toward the late 1870s, the family moved to Halstead, Kansas, for a short time. There, Emerson again worked on the farm and shot prairie chickens to provide meat for the family. He recalled in his autobiography, "I would take the gun to the field and the prairie chickens would be walking around where we were plowing, and when I went to go home I would take the gun and pick out which ever chicken I wanted and shoot it and take it home with me."[17]

During the fall of 1880, Emerson moved back to McPherson County and went to a country school in the Spring Valley district. At some point during this time, Emerson boarded with Cell Law, working for his room and board. In his autobiography, Emerson reflected, "Mr. Law wanted me to work for him but he wanted me to work for $17 per month and I wanted $18. This may have been a turning point in my life. I took my earthly effects in my arm, which as I remember it, were very few and walked across the country to Hutchinson. I had no money to buy a ticket on the railroad at that time. We lived in town and I did team work, plowing gardens, hauling dirt, etc."

Emerson harvested for William Astle near Haven, Kansas, in 1881 and the next year went to school in Hutchinson. He studied under two illustrious teachers, Mr. A.W. McCandless and Dr. George Winans.[18] McCandless continued teaching for many years and was on the board of education for over thirty-eight years. Winans was the city schools' superintendent for over ten years. These two teachers would later have two schools named

A very young Emerson, circa 1881. *Mike Carey Collection.*

after them in Hutchinson.[19] Although Emerson's formal education was spotty at best, maybe having been taught for even a couple of years by these devoted education professionals ingrained and reinforced in him a love for lifelong learning that helped him to excel.

Around 1882, one day while on Main Street in Hutchinson, Emerson stopped to admire the tall, two-story buildings. Noticing the strapping young man gazing up at the buildings, a man offered Emerson work on his farm in Valley Township. Emerson accepted and soon began to work for this man, Marshall Hale. He completed the required work that Hale had set out for him in half the time expected, greatly impressing Hale. Soon afterward, Hale offered Emerson a position in his coal, building material and hide merchant business in 1883. Hale paid Emerson twenty-five dollars per month as starting pay. Emerson drove mule teams, delivering coal and building materials to customers and receiving payments. Hale had a distrust of banking institutions and kept all his money in a pocketbook. Emerson related the story of how he learned a lesson to keep track of money while working for Hale. He lost Hale's pocketbook containing sixty-five dollars and had to pay it back month to month out of his small wages. He even managed to save a small portion out of his wages to send to his family in Halstead. He did this by being frugal with his lifestyle at the time, even to the point that Emerson slept in the office of the coal yard. Frugality was to be a way of life for Emerson.[20]

Finally, as a young adult of the age of twenty, all the moving around that Emerson had experienced as a young child began to wear on him. Returning home one evening after a hard day's work, Emerson peered in the windows of the lovely homes in Hutchinson and noticed other stable, well-off families enjoying bountiful meals. He compared their meals with those of his own family. He thought, "Why is it that other children can have all those nice things, and my brothers and sisters have to do without them? Suddenly the answer came to me: There I was, waiting for something good to happen to me, instead of digging it out for myself. I knew that Lincoln would never have been satisfied with that."[21] In this moment of clarity, Emerson's life was about to change dramatically.

Chapter 2

EMERSON'S EMPIRE BEGINS

1882–1895

D uring 1884, Hale intended to sell his coal business to John Duckworth, and having Emerson as an employee was a selling point. However, with his new outlook on life, Emerson had reached a point where he would no longer consent to work for others but would be master of his own business. Emerson approached an acquaintance, R.E. Conn, to provide the capital for his own coal venture. Conn quickly agreed because after observing Emerson for quite some time, he believed that Emerson had the potential to become so much more than he was.[22] Upon hearing about Emerson's budding partnership with Conn, Hale attempted to thwart the new business by threatening to accuse Emerson of improper accounting in Hale's books. Conn took no stock in Hale's accusations, and thus, the new business of Conn and Carey, which was located at the corner of Avenue B and Main Street, was formed.[23] The November 29, 1884 issue of the *Hutchinson Herald* officially announced that "Conn and Carey have formed a partnership handling coal, lime, hair, and hides."[24] Conn supplied the working capital of just over $300, and Carey supplied the experience.[25] Conn worked in the office, and Carey handled deliveries and sold the coal, building materials and hides. The first year, Conn and Carey had profits of $2,700. Emerson's half of this profit was more than twice what he had made working for Hale. To the end of his life, Emerson never forgot Hale's attempt to slander his good character.[26]

Having a good character and high integrity and being community minded were, in fact, very important to Emerson. In 1885, the citizens of

Hutchinson raised $25,000 to buy land on which a state reformatory could be built. Emerson was very proud of the fact that his very first philanthropic contribution was $25 that he gave toward this cause.[27]

Profits at Conn and Carey rose to about $3,300 in 1886.[28] Emerson must have felt successful and confident this year because he quickly became involved in many activities outside his business and immersed himself in a variety of community organizations. He joined the fraternal organization Knights of Pythias, also known locally as the K.P. Lodge. There, twenty-three-year-old Emerson held the position of the keeper of records and seals.[29]

Also, in 1886, Emerson showed additional early signs of becoming an involved and caring community member when he joined the Hutchinson Fire Department. The "Kids" and "Dudes" were two volunteer firefighting companies that year. Captain Joe Krenrich, a furniture dealer, led the Kids, which consisted of school boys. Captain George Steit led the Dudes, a company of young professionals. The two companies also formed opposing baseball teams and were very competitive, both in firefighting and on the baseball diamond. It's no wonder Emerson became involved with both firefighting and baseball. As a young, upcoming professional in Reno County, Emerson naturally was a member of the Dudes company. For the Dudes' baseball team, he played catcher. At first, all the firefighters were volunteers. Eventually, the city council paid each man three dollars to replace their clothes. As an added incentive, the council paid ten dollars to the first hose company to arrive on the scene of a fire. This incentive soon became too expensive when the number of fires mysteriously began to escalate. The Kids were always the first to arrive on the scene. No formal charges were ever filed, but the Dudes could not understand how the Kids were always first to every fire. In August 1886, the Dudes played in a baseball game versus the Kids. Emerson played catcher in that game. The Dudes were victorious, winning 23–6.[30] Still volunteering for the fire department in 1887, Emerson was a driver for Company Number 1.[31]

Emerson enjoyed success both on the baseball field and in his business partnership with Conn. With the profits from their successful business, in 1887 Emerson took the first vacation of his lifetime in a covered wagon, touring the timber and mining industries of Arkansas. He must have been quite impressed with resources in Arkansas because during this time, he and W.E. Hutchinson (a local Hutchinson banker and cousin of Hutchinson founder Clinton Carter "C.C." Hutchinson) purchased a coal mine in Russellville, Arkansas. Emerson's brother Arthur became the mine superintendent. The Carey Coal and Mining Company was part of the Ouita coal field and sold a type of coal known as Bernice coal. Emerson was only involved with the Arkansas mine for a couple of years because it was unprofitable due to lack of railroad regulations at the time leading to a scarcity of available rail cars for shipping. He sold his half interest in the business to Hutchinson, losing $1,800 in the venture. Emerson chalked it up to a lesson learned, stating, "I find experience is a dear teacher, but I am firm in the opinion that the old adage is correct that 'fools will learn in no other way.'"[32]

Things were also starting to boom for Reno County. In 1887, a land developer for the Santa Fe Railroad plotted out the city of South Hutchinson. His name was Ben Blanchard, and he thought that if he found oil in South Hutchinson, he could sell his plots more easily, so he began drilling a well. At about 350 feet, he hit a white substance—salt. Soon salt companies began to spring up like dandelions. By 1888, there were ten in Reno County.[33] It seemed as though any entrepreneur with enough money to afford to sink a well 650 feet deep started a salt company. These salt plants were simple operations using pans and coal fires to dry saline water extracted from these wells, commonly called brine wells, to recover the salt.[34] The salt boom of 1888 had begun, and along with it came a boom in the demand for building materials and coal.

Emerson stands tall near the campfire on his trip to Arkansas in 1887. *Conard-Harmon Collection.*

Emerson traveled to Arkansas on his first vacation ever in 1887. Emerson is the third man from the right. *Conard-Harmon Collection.*

Conn jumped onto the salt boom bandwagon and formed an association with other investors building the Star Salt Plant on the west end of Hutchinson. Subsequently, Conn sold off his portion of the coal company to two men, Herman Beers and Albert Lee. The coal company then became known as Carey, Beers, and Lee, and during 1888 and 1889, profits soared to about $10,000.[35]

Enjoying his newly found wealth, Emerson had been dabbling in land purchases. In November 1887, Emerson had purchased Samuel's property at lot 55 on East Avenue B. This empty lot was across the street from Samuel's home at 214 East Avenue B. This may have been because of the land boom that was going on at the time in Kansas. It could have been simply to help his father with some cash. For whatever reason, it was recorded in the *Hutchinson Daily News* as a land transfer from Samuel to Emerson for $1,600. This was a grand sum in 1887, which indicates that Emerson was willing to speculate in land and that he was flush with cash. In March 1888, Emerson sold some land in the Sunflower Town Addition to a J.C. Hutchinson for $1,050. Then in June 1888, he bought some land for $700, turned it around and sold it for $1,200 on the same day, according to the land transfers. The boom was on, and Emerson was in the thick of it.[36]

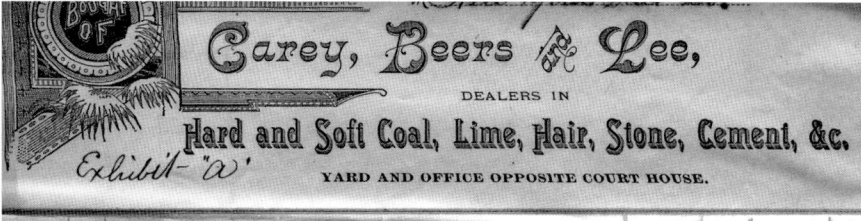

The ornate letterhead of this 1888 Carey, Beers, and Lee receipt is a perfect example of Emerson's pride that he had in his company. *Reno County Museum Collection.*

Now living with his family at 214 East Avenue B in Hutchinson proper, 1888 was a whirlwind year for Emerson. Already heavily involved in community organizations and activities, Emerson was instrumental in securing a semi-professional baseball club in Hutchinson that was part of the Western League. He was the president of the club. The team played at a park between 12th and 14th Streets, east of Main Street; however, the team never gained successful momentum and failed to complete a whole season.[37] If all of those activities weren't enough, Emerson was also elected as treasurer of the Hutchinson chess club.[38] During this same year, the sport of coursing (dog and horse hunting by sight rather than scent) took off in Hutchinson under the direction of John R. Price of Topeka, M.E. Allison, W.L. Woodnutt and J.A. Myers. This group of gentlemen heavily promoted bringing the sport of coursing to Hutchinson. The secretary of state in Topeka, Kansas, granted a charter to the National Coursing Association to create a Hutchinson chapter. A total of $50,000 of Hutchinson capital stock was used to purchase ground on which to establish the first enclosed coursing park in the United States. There were even plans for a ten-thousand-seat grandstand to be built, and the track was to be three-quarters of a mile long by two hundred yards wide. Always wanting to be involved and on the forefront of the action, Emerson served as secretary for this Hutchinson chapter.[39]

An even more—perhaps the most—important event for Emerson in 1888 was his marriage to Anna May Puterbaugh on September 27.[40] Anna May was the daughter of Olive V. and John Puterbaugh, who had just passed away of a heart attack in Topeka, Kansas, in March 1888. This blending of families would create a powerful base in the future. Emerson described Anna May as having "a wonderful intellect, a splendid education, high ideals, and a non-compromising moral standard." Well on his way to becoming a successful family man at the ripe old age of twenty-five, Emerson built a fine two-story, four-room house in the 1000 block of North Main Street.[41]

Above: *Back row from left*: Emerson's oldest son, Howard Jay; wife, Anna May (Puterbaugh); Emerson; J.G. Puterbaugh (Anna May's brother); possibly Mabel Puterbaugh or one of the Puterbaugh brothers' wives. *Middle row from left*: Probably W.D. (Will) Puterbaugh; possibly Mabel or other wife; Olive Puterbaugh (Emerson's mother-in-law); possibly Mabel or a Puterbaugh wife; possibly John Puterbaugh *Front row from left*: Emerson's other three sons: Charles E.; William David (W.D.P.); Emerson Jr. (June). The photo was taken circa 1907. *Mike Carey Collection.*

Right: Anna May Puterbaugh Carey, about 1900. *Conard-Harmon Collection.*

Business boomed throughout Hutchinson during the remainder of the year. More and more salt companies sprang up, new buildings were being built and commerce bustled along. Just some of the industries that exploded in 1888 were the Hutchinson Salt Manufacturing Company, the Diamond Salt Company, the Hutchinson Soap Factory and the Hutchinson Flour Milling Company. All these new companies and new buildings needed coal for heating and all manner of building materials, which Emerson's company was only happily willing to supply. In fact, Emerson's coal company was just one of nine companies that sold coal exclusively that year; there were even five more that sold feed and coal. The Carey, Beers, and Lee Coal Company had stiff competition. However, Carey, Beers, and Lee thrived and grew accordingly.[42]

Flush with the success of the coal company, Emerson turned to even more outside interests. The Oklahoma land grab was on with a vengeance. Two million acres of land were opened to settlement, combined with the earlier Homestead Act of 1862, and the stage was set for a mass rush of human greed as pioneers poured into the Oklahoma territories. Around fifty thousand hopeful pioneers, the "boomers," came rushing into Oklahoma in April 1889.[43] Emerson was one of those fifty thousand. Claiming to be just curious, he went "more to see what was going on than anything else." Emerson bought a brand-new striped silk shirt and a new coat to explore the newly opened land in Guthrie. He traveled with Mr. T.J. Anderson. He planned to stay in Oklahoma for only one day and so traveled light. Upon arriving in Guthrie, Emerson chose a lot between the Santa Fe Depot and Main Street and staked out the area with a newly purchased wagon cover he used for a tent. A group of other prospectors from Hutchinson, intent on setting up a restaurant in the new land, joined up with Emerson, and soon his lot became the Hutchinson contingent's headquarters. Throughout the day, fights and skirmishes broke out as the ownership of lots was highly contested. It became so congested that homesteaders could barely walk through the streets due to the massive numbers of tents that had sprang up to stake claims. Several claim jumpers attempted to steal Emerson's lot; however, with the help of all those in the Hutchinson party, Emerson managed to scare them off, maintaining constant possession of his lot for ten days. After constructing a $500 building, Emerson eventually sold his lot to Bob Wright of Dodge City thirty days later for a profit of $1,010.[44]

Emerson returned home victorious from his travels in Oklahoma. Perhaps it is for this reason that during 1889, Emerson bought out his partners, Beers and Lee, for twice what they originally had paid for Conn's share. The business became the Carey Coal Company and further reinforced Emerson's driving need to be the sole owner of his own company.[45]

However, there were dark clouds on the horizon, for as quickly as the dandelions had grown, their demise was just as quick. Beginning in 1889, Emerson explained, "When the boom failed it was just as if a bubble had been pierced. Prosperity vanished into thin air." This bust hit Hutchinson hard, and Emerson fell hard right along with it. During the boom years, Emerson had borrowed heavily and found himself about $15,000 in debt. On the advice of his banker, Emerson had reinvested his profits instead of paying off his loans. As a result, when the bubble burst, he was forced to sell everything he owned to make good on his debts. Although his home was exempt by law and safe from creditors, Emerson made the decision to sell it to fully repay all his loans and keep his company intact. He and Anna were forced to rent a little house at 223 West 11th Avenue for $6.25 per month. Emerson stated that he had learned two valuable lessons in business from this difficult episode in his life: "Never borrow money to buy something that you don't need," and "Remember that, nine times out of ten, a poor man cannot afford to pay interest."[46] Emerson took much pride in fully paying off his debts. In his autobiography, Emerson proudly states that unlike his ex-partners, Beers and Lee, who paid off their debts with "mule shoes," he paid off his debts "100 cents on the dollar."[47]

Now with much less fluid income and a more cautious and resolute attitude, Emerson would have surely turned his sights to his family and concentrated his efforts on stabilizing his core business. On July 28, 1891, Emerson and Anna must have been overjoyed when their first son, Howard J., was born.[48] By 1891, the success of the return to prosperity of the Carey Coal Company was evidenced as Emerson was appointed the general agent of his coal supplier, the Kansas and Texas Coal Company.[49] Emerson advertised in the *Semi-Weekly Gazette* on January 23, 1891:

> *I have just completed an office and coal bins on Third avenue east, near Main street, on the Santa Fe tracks, which I opened for business on Monday. Being located as I am on "track" thus doing away with any expense of hauling, etc., I will be able to handle coal 10 cents per ton cheaper than before, which I propose to give to the consumer. The following are prices at yard:*
> *Anthracite, $10 05.*
> *Canon City, No. 1, $6 40.*
> *Canon City, No. 7, $6 00.*

Weir, lump, $4 15.
Weir, nut, $3 90.
Osage shaft, $4 00.
The following extra charge will be made for drayage: Per ton 35 cents;
half ton, 25 cents; 500 pounds or less, 15 cents.
All coal will be screened perfectly clean and just as many pounds as you
pay for. I appreciate the liberal patronage I have had during the many years
I have been in business in Hutchinson, and in return promise to be here
many years more, seeing that you get good clean coal, just what you buy, and
that very cheap, barring providential hinderances [sic].

Respectfully,
Emerson Carey

Now he supplied coal and building materials not only to Hutchinson but also to all of Kansas. The expanded coal wholesale business employed four teams locally and two salesmen statewide. Emerson also achieved success in the hide business; however, in 1893, the Carey Hide Company split off and became the Kansas Hide Company.[50] This separation of companies shows Emerson's wisdom, which was learned from the near crash of the coal and hide company. Now, if one company failed, the others could succeed unimpeded. Emerson had really grasped the concept of diversification.

Children were coming quickly now, and on July 9, 1893, their second son, Charles E., was born.[51] Growing up in a family full of sisters, Emerson certainly had to be thrilled that his first two children were boys. Unfortunately, when Charles was about six months old, Anna May became afflicted with rheumatism. She was confined to her bed for the vast part of six months, and Emerson took care of Charles in the evenings after business hours. He bought "an old-fashioned phaeton for her [Anna May] to take a little air and sunshine in." (The phaeton was a horse-drawn, open-air carriage with oversized wheels.) Sometime later, Emerson took Anna to Hot Springs, Arkansas, for about six weeks to help her recuperate, while Charles remained with his grandmother.[52] With his wife improving, but not in the best of health, his two new sons, his growing business and all his community obligations, it seemed Emerson would have had little time for the pursuit of new ventures.

However, Emerson chartered the Hutchinson Fuel and Hide Company in 1893. The directors were Arthur Carey, Samuel Carey, Jay G. Puterbaugh, William D. Puterbaugh and Emerson Carey. The charter was notarized in

Pope County, Arkansas—the same county as Russellville, Arkansas, where Emerson and W.E. Hutchinson owned the coal mine.[53] It seems rather certain that the Hutchinson Fuel and Hide Company was created as both the selling and wholesaling arm of Carey Coal. Emerson would have wanted to sell coal directly in Arkansas, and he needed a way to wholesale coal to coal dealers; how better to do this than by changing the name of the wholesaler? This made it seem less intrusive than Carey Coal, which had existed in Hutchinson for quite some time by then.

Unbelievably, while Emerson ran the coal and hide businesses and had a growing family, he continued to farm extensively. Throughout this time, he had four hundred head of cattle and 2,500 sheep. He also partnered with Mr. C.W. Southward and fed 14,000 sheep north of Hutchinson. The partners netted fifty cents per head profit, which split equally between the two men would have been about $3,500 each.[54]

Emerson's explosive expansion into industry must have required an incredible amount of funding, and so he and Anna May took out a hefty combination of mortgages with the Valley State Bank, located on the corner of Main Street and Sherman. The 1893 mortgages were signed by the vice president of the bank, who was none other than Emerson's traveling and business partner, W.E. Hutchinson. The chattel mortgage lists the following personal property items that were in Emerson and Anna's possession at the time of the mortgage:

63 shoats (young pigs), at 130 pounds each
7 shoats, 60 pounds each
240 shoats, 100 pounds each
411 brood sows, about 200 pounds each
3 pigs
10 brood sows
1 boar & 5 suckling pigs
2 red cows
1 heifer
1 red & white ox
1 sorrel colt
3 gray colts
1 black colt
3 bay colts
1 lumber wagon, with box and hay rack
1 mowing machine and horse rake

2 iron gray mares, 3 mules, 1 sorrel pony
1 bay mare named "Nellie"; 1 bay horse named "Frank"; 1 gray horse named "Sam"; 1 iron gray horse named "Prince"

Other properties listed on the mortgage were three office scales, a warehouse, a coal house and all the buildings on land that Emerson leased at 94 and 96 South Main Street. The parcels that Emerson owned included in the land portion of the mortgage were listed as

SE quarter of section twenty-seven (27), township twenty-two (22), range five (5), west
Lot one (1), section twenty-five (25), township twenty-three (23), range six (6), west
Lot eleven (11), Avenue "C" East in the City of Hutchinson, Kansas

The mortgage value listed for all the above properties was $2,000, $1,800 and $500, respectively, for a total of $4,300. (This would be $124,500 figuring in today's inflation.)[55]

Left to right: Samuel Carey, Emerson Carey, unknown and Mr. Young stand in front of Young's blacksmith shop on the north side of Avenue B in 1896. *Reno County Museum Collection.*

The Carey-Puterbaugh Coal office building was only a crude building at 12–16 East 3rd Avenue, about 1893. *Conard-Harmon Collection.*

Even with the mortgage he took out and possibly because of his expansion into the ice business, Emerson needed more capital and management personnel he could trust. Emerson reorganized the Carey Coal Company into the Carey-Puterbaugh Coal Company on September 28, 1894, with Emerson serving as president; his brother Arthur as vice president and manager; J.G. Puterbaugh, Emerson's brother-in-law, as secretary; and Emerson's father, Samuel Carey, as treasurer.[56] The office was located on East 3rd Avenue, while the coal yard itself was located at 310 South Main. The Carey-Puterbaugh Coal Company was an exclusive selling agent for the Missouri Pacific Company's coal, whose specialty was Eureka anthracite.[57]

In December 1893, Emerson showed both his generosity and wit when, on December 24, he gave all his employees "a large fat juicy gobbler" for Christmas dinner. On the same day, he left the *Hutchinson Daily News* a lump of his best Denning coal.[58]

CHAPTER 3

COLD CASH

1896–1900

However, other interests still called to Emerson, and in 1896, with his seemingly endless amounts of energy, he plunged into the ice manufacturing business. He rented the Underwood Packing Company under the impression that it was a full-fledged ice-making plant, but it was only a refrigeration plant. Emerson invested heavily to convert the 226 South Main facility into an ice-manufacturing plant, and so by 1897, the Hutchinson Ice Company was born. Emerson recalled, "I made no money but gained a world of experience and earned enough to reimburse me for the outlay."[59] At this time, the ice company was producing ten tons of ice each day.[60] The process for making ice at this time was to generate steam, which was then used to drive a steam engine. The steam engine, in turn, then drove a compressor, which compressed ammonia gas that cooled the ice plant. It's likely that Emerson used waste coal from his coal operations to fire his boilers that generated the steam to make the ice.[61]

Emerson ran multiple ads in the local paper designed to undersell any competitors: "Until further notice I will sell ice cheap at my plant at ten cents per one hundred pounds in any quantity from fifty pounds up. Why pay twenty cents to twenty-five cents per one hundred pounds for ice? Drive to my plant and get ice cheap. Emerson Carey."[62]

Ice was important to have along the rail lines because it was used by the railroad companies to cool down refrigerated rail cars. Emerson was surely aware of this fact. These cars were developed by meatpacking companies to enable delivery of carcasses nationwide. A deep layer of ice was spread

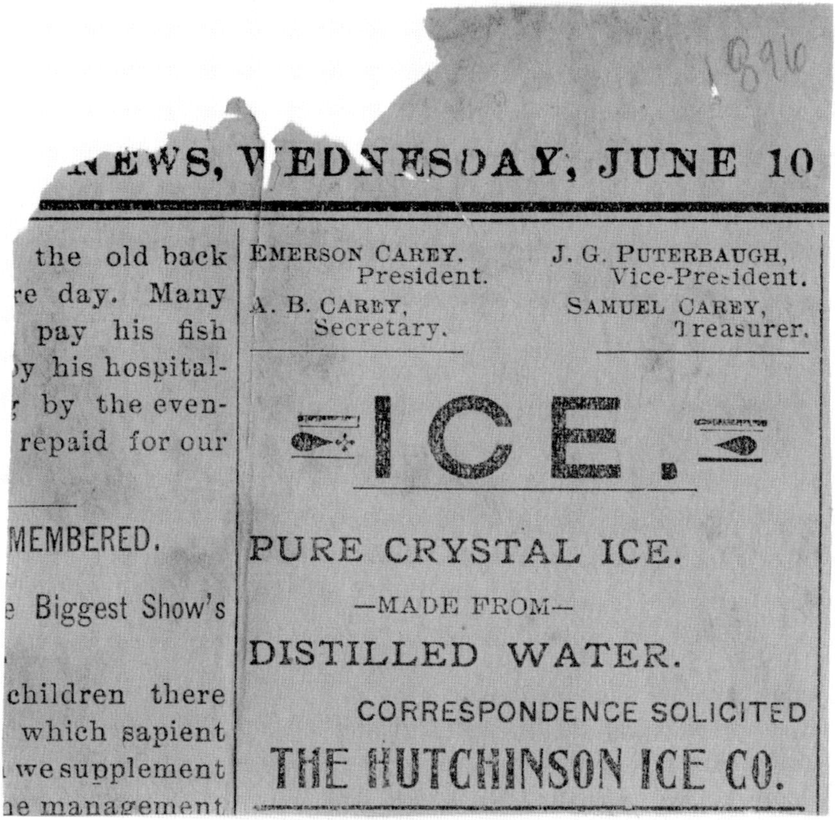

1896

NEWS, WEDNESDAY, JUNE 10

the old back | EMERSON CAREY. President. | J. G. PUTERBAUGH, Vice-President.
re day. Many | A. B. CAREY, Secretary. | SAMUEL CAREY, Treasurer.
pay his fish
by his hospital-
by the even-
repaid for our

ICE.

PURE CRYSTAL ICE.

MEMBERED.

e Biggest Show's

children there
which sapient
we supplement
he management.

—MADE FROM—

DISTILLED WATER.

CORRESPONDENCE SOLICITED

THE HUTCHINSON ICE CO.

Upper management was kept "all in the family" in Emerson's Hutchinson Ice Company, as shown in this early advertisement. *Reno County Museum Collection.*

on the floor of the refrigeration car, and a layer of salt was placed on top of the ice to make it even colder. These cars would have to stop and re-ice from time to time. Another method for cooling the cars used bins on the ends that allowed air from the outside to run through the ice and chill the air. Fruits and vegetables also were iced down on cross-country trips. The use of salt in this process may have played a factor in Emerson's future business developments.[63]

Electrical power was a new science in the 1890s, and Emerson was eager to try new technologies. In early 1896, Emerson purchased a generator and used the mechanical power from his steam engine to operate it.[64] He was already producing the steam and mechanical power to operate his

Looking east from Main, a Carey Coal Company ice wagon wades through 1st Street during one of Hutchinson's many floods. *Conard-Harmon Collection.*

The original generator used in the Carey Industries, most probably used in the ice industry, now makes its home at the Reno County Museum. *Reno County Museum Collection.*

ammonia compressors for his ice plant. This really illustrated Emerson's resourcefulness, frugality and ingenuity. One can speculate that Emerson would have used waste coal, yet again, to make steam and waste mechanical power to make electricity. The electrical power produced by this generator was used in the ice plant and would be crucial in Emerson's later ventures.

Although Emerson's business interests were back on track, 1896 brought sadness once more into the Carey family when, on July 2, Emerson's mother, Nancy Jane Bundy Carey, died at the age of fifty-four.[65] Her youngest boy, Emerson's brother Claude, was ten years old, and Nancy had spent almost half of her life giving birth to Emerson's twelve siblings. It's a fair assumption that Nancy endured a harsh, difficult life during many of those early years, and it's a testament to her strength that she raised such a large and thriving family. Nancy was laid to rest in Eastside Cemetery in Hutchinson, Kansas.[66]

It's also an indication of Emerson's tenacity that not even the passing of his mother could suppress his spirit and drive to excel. One year later, in 1897, Emerson and other stockholders incorporated the Hutchinson Street Railway Company.[67] At this time, it was still a horse-drawn trolley system running throughout the city, providing mass transportation to a growing urban population and city center. Businesses were showing signs of rebounding from an early financial bust of 1893, and there were doctors to visit, lawyers to meet, shopping to be done, business to be taken care of—all downtown. Additionally, as early as 1887, the street railway traveled to Riverside Park, which was at the south end of Main Street and ran along one side of the Arkansas River. The railway owned this roughly fifty acres of land and by 1888 already was home to a small zoological garden consisting of eagles, antelope and other animals. Riverside Park also had large trees, gravel walkways, brightly planted flower beds, an ice cream pavilion and a music stand.[68] The official incorporation of the railway utilized this very convenient ownership of the park as a natural customer base for the railway; riders flocked to the railway to visit the recently improved park. Early on, Emerson saw the need for inner-city transportation and quickly hopped aboard the train. He may not have known it at the time, but this first step aboard the trolley led him to a more important transportation venture in the future.

Another early entrepreneur was Charles S. Winchester, who in 1893 opened his Old Fulton Market, a retail meat business, at 409 South Main. As his meat business expanded and with Emerson's collaboration, they built a packinghouse on South Main in October 1898. The company was already being referred to as the Carey-Winchester Packing Company. The two

Emerson Carey, circa 1898.
Reno County Museum Collection.

William David Puterbaugh,
Anna's brother and Emerson's
brother-in-law. *Conard-Harmon
Collection.*

families were well associated, as Charles's only son, S. Allen, initially worked for five years for Emerson in the coal and hide company.[69]

Having established his ice-making company, Emerson made the natural transition in 1898 to a cold storage facility. He quickly enlarged the cold storage facility in 1899 and changed the company's name to the Hutchinson Ice and Cold Storage Company.[70]

Winchester wasn't the only early entrepreneur Emerson was involved with during this period. In 1900, a group of Hutchinson's movers and shakers began making plans for a city park. The chairman of the group was Edward Moore, and the secretary was John Kinkel. Others in the group besides Emerson were J.U. Brown, L.A. Beebe, Houston Whiteside and A.N. Brown, among others. This group of men discussed the rules and regulations of the park organization. At this time, their dreams were to develop a park including a 240-acre tract of land with a baseball diamond in the center and an auditorium capable of housing large indoor meetings. This farsighted group envisioned what Hutchinson could become by capitalizing on the momentum of success currently coursing through the city. They also hoped that the park would provide yet more business for the street railway company.[71]

While Emerson worked on organizing a city park, his father, Samuel, was active in city affairs as well. He took an interest in politics, beginning with a run on the local school board. Next, Samuel ran successfully as an Independent against Republican candidate H.S. Schall for an open Fourth Ward council post.[72] It seems that it would be very unlikely that Samuel would have run for city commission without Emerson's encouragement. Perhaps Emerson wanted someone on the inside whom he could trust, and that would be none other than his father. It is obvious that Samuel took many cues from Emerson, as he sat on the boards of most of Emerson's early companies. So, while there is no direct evidence that Emerson was behind Samuel's foray into politics, it seems most likely. It's possible, also, that Emerson would soon capitalize on having his father be a political insider.

While Emerson surely had to have closely followed the political aspirations of his father, it's certain that his attention was happily diverted by the birth of his third child. William David Puterbaugh (W.D.P.) Carey was born on September 4, 1901. W.D.P. was named after his uncle, Anna May's brother, William David Puterbaugh.[73] Emerson must have been delighted to be blessed with three sons. Emerson and Anna May's sons were destined to be fully engaged in and contributors to the overall success in Emerson's life.

Chapter 4

SALT BANDWAGON

1901–1905

The dawn of a new century must have been an incredibly exciting time. The hope of the twentieth century beckoned, and Emerson responded with even more expansion to his empire. By now, the salt companies in Hutchinson were producing substantial amounts of salt through the simple evaporation method. Emerson noted that in 1901, there were fifty salt companies in the midwestern area, and in Hutchinson alone, there were five salt companies.[74] Seeing the success of the salt producers all around him, Emerson plunged headfirst into the business that was soon to become synonymous with the Carey name. On April 18, Emerson contracted with C.L. Bloom, president of the Independent Gas Company, to dig a well at his ice plant. The well would supply the water for Emerson's latest business venture: his salt-producing company. The water from this well also supplied water for what was known as "The Beach" or Emerson's natatorium. The Beach was a one-hundred-by-two-hundred-foot free public bathing pool for Hutchinson's citizens. It had its own bathhouses and was located on the corner of Avenue C and Walnut, just east of Emerson's ice plant. A much smaller example of his generosity, the Beach was just another way in which Emerson gave back to the city.[75]

Never one to waste anything, Emerson realized that the waste steam from his ice company, as mentioned earlier, could be used to heat salt pans to evaporate brine into salt.[76] Directly as a result of his frugality and resourcefulness, on April 25, 1901, the new Carey Salt Company became a family affair with Emerson as president, of course; C.W. Southward

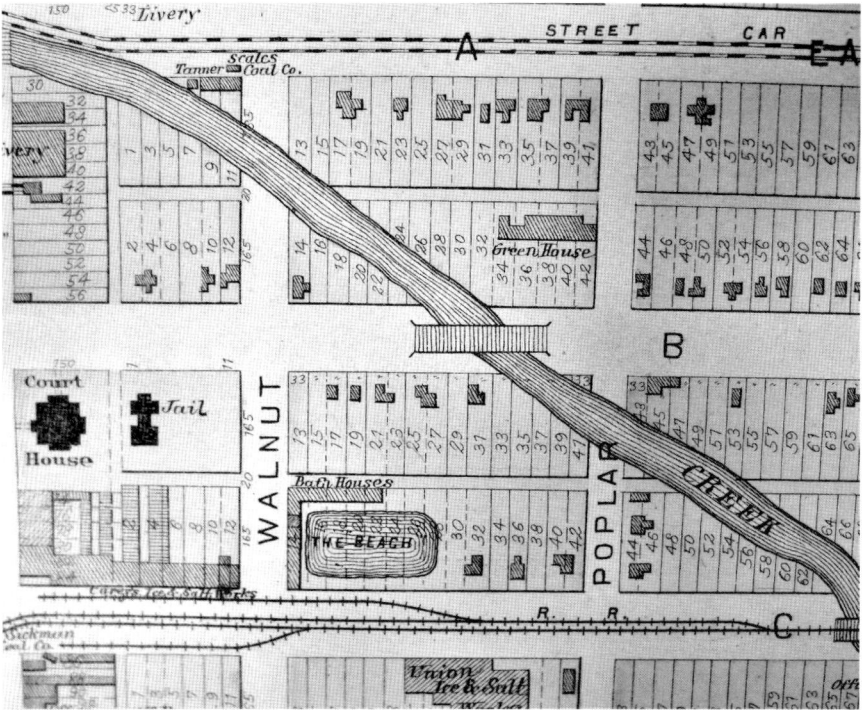

The "Beach" with its bathhouses was located just east of Emerson's salt and cold storage companies at Walnut and Avenue C in 1902. *Reno County Museum Collection.*

as vice president; Emerson's sister Edith as secretary, stenographer and bookkeeper; and W.D. Puterbaugh (his brother-in-law) as treasurer.[77] Emerson's new venture into salt production was initially a two-pan plant located at the corner of Avenue C and Main Street toward the south end of Hutchinson. Emerson must have been extremely excited and gratified when he shipped out that first rail car of salt in July 1901 to the Baden Produce Company of Winfield, Kansas.[78] Emerson's Carey Salt Company was the last salt company to jump onto the Hutchinson salt bandwagon, but certainly not the least.

This newcomer to the salt business made quite the impression in Hutchinson. An article in the *Saturday Bee* on November 29, 1902, called Emerson a "hustler" and noted that "his business on South Main is one of the Big Things in Town." The article urged the reader to go inspect Emerson's new business. "It is worth anyone's time to go down to the Carey Plant and see how he turns blue-looking water into salt that is 98 percent pure

The Carey Coal Company operation at 310 South Main with ice plant and the early Carey Salt Company, around 1901. *Reno County Museum Collection.*

or even a little more so if possible."[79] Emerson lost no time in capitalizing on this sparkling new product and, by extension, the reputation it afforded him.

He collaborated with the Home Theatre owner Mr. Casner in 1902 to pave their portion of Main Street with a combination of salt and cinders. This is something that had been done successfully before, but to the detriment of all the vegetation and shade trees in the area. The county took note of Emerson's "hustle" and in 1902 awarded him the coal contract to supply coal for the county courthouse, the jail, the county farm and the poor of Reno County. This contract alone was worth an estimated $1,000 and possibly more each year. (This is the equivalent of about $29,000 in today's inflationary market.) The *Weekly Interior Herald* newspaper even noted that "the Carey Salt Company uses the most beautiful and expensive office stationery to be had anywhere. It is of such character as to be the envy of any business man taking pride in the appearance of his outgoing mail. Mr. Carey always did have a great deal of pride."[80]

That same year, Emerson was determined to make the new Carey Salt Company work. He proved this by refusing to bow to possibly trumped-up fire code violations. In 1900, the city passed some controversial fire ordinances. Often referred to as the "fire trap ordinance," it was designed to prevent the construction of fire trap buildings. Fire trap buildings were large, balloon-framed structures, such as barns. The buildings were seen as difficult to extinguish once a fire started with the limited resources the city had at the time. The ordinance was highly controversial and challenged by several commercial business owners. This happened early on in the ordinance's life when construction of a barn was started right before the ordinance was passed. The city allowed the barn to be finished. This action made other business owners believe that if construction of a building began before the ordinance was passed, it could then be added onto without following the ordinance, with no repercussion by the city.[81] Emerson was aware of this, and so in 1902, he added on to his existing building to expand his salt plant. As a result, the city set a warrant for Emerson, and he was arrested. Emerson soon bailed out and was fined by police court $25. The very next day, as Emerson continued to build, the city issued another warrant. This happened numerous times while expanding the new salt plant. It occurred so much that the *Hutchinson News* exclaimed that if this continued to happen, Emerson would "pay $9,000 in a year to add a room to the plant." After each arrest, Emerson bonded out of jail and continued his business growth. This cycle of arrest and bonding reportedly continued until the city grew tired of it and left him alone.[82]

This may have been one of his first tangles with the powerful salt trust. The salt trust was a group of nine companies headed by Joy Morton, president of the Morton Salt Company of Chicago. The salt trust set production limits and prices in the Hutchinson salt market. Morton bought or froze out other salt companies in Hutchinson to gain customers and eliminate competition. Emerson said, "Mr. Morton seemed to be possessed of the idea that he should do all the business."[83] Emerson aligned his salt company with the other independent salt companies at the time, which included the Hutchinson Pure Salt Company, Union Ice and Salt Company and Barton Salt Company.[84]

In this early photograph, circa 1906, the Morton Salt Plant, owned by Emerson's arch rival Joy Morton, is just being built. *Reno County Museum Collection.*

Frank Vincent, president of the Hutchinson-Kansas Salt Company (which was part of the salt trust) and repeat mayor of Hutchinson. *Reno County Museum Collection.*

Feeling threatened by the growth of the Carey Salt Company, the president of the Hutchinson-Kansas Salt Company, Frank Vincent (who served as mayor of Hutchinson ten times throughout the years of 1892 to 1918), paid a visit to Emerson. The Hutchinson-Kansas Salt Company was part of the salt trust. Vincent encouraged Emerson to sell his salt business to the trust, intimating that it would be in Emerson's best interest. Vincent backed up his intimidation by promising to flood the market with thousands of barrels of salt, thereby dropping prices and forcing Emerson to quit the salt business. Emerson responded by saying, "Go ahead and do the worst you can do....I have seen many a fly make a bull waggle its tail."[85]

Making good on the threat, the Hutchinson-Kansas Salt Company did flood the market, and the price per barrel went from eighty-five cents to fifty-five cents. Carey Salt sold its salt as low as forty-five cents per barrel, which Emerson noted was less than the cost of producing the salt itself. He explained, "Our business was so hooked up, however, with ice, salt, cold storage, and coal business that we never showed a loss in any month." Eventually, the extremely low price per barrel caused a glut of ordering, and both the Carey Salt Company and salt trust companies fell behind fulfilling orders. Emerson's strategy of hanging on and not giving in forced the salt trust to capitulate, and prices slowly began to rise once again.[86]

Interestingly, Emerson's fight with the salt trust was very typical of the fights between other cutthroat, industrialist magnates at the time. Emerson attributed his responsive actions toward the salt trust's intimidations to a man from Chicago in the steel business. While in Chicago to purchase a boiler for his new salt company, Emerson shared his experiences with the steel man. This businessman had himself recently tangled with the steel trust in Chicago. The unnamed man then related, step by step, exactly what Morton and Vincent would proceed to do to drive Emerson out of business. The man explained that Morton would first offer to buy the Carey Salt Company, then would lower prices of his product to ridiculously low prices and finally Morton would attempt to offer the proverbial olive branch by asking Emerson to cooperate in leveling out the price of salt between the two companies. Emerson noted that these "were just exactly the steps that followed my advent into the salt business."[87]

With the salt battle abating somewhat at this time, Emerson explored new options for his salt products. One such offering was a smaller, lighter-weight twenty-five-pound sack of salt, which became very popular.[88] This is evidence that very early in Emerson's career, he adopted innovative methods of marketing his salt products.

Emerson began building a new cold storage facility at the south end of the city on July 10, 1902. It was to be 80 feet by 80 feet, two stories high and made of pressed red brick. The final completed structure would have 128,000 cubic feet of storage for fruits and vegetables and would contain no windows to let out any of the cold. He moved his coal and brick yards to the area once known as the "Carey Beach." Thus, the impromptu swimming area came to an end in 1902. At this time, between Emerson's coal, ice and salt plants, he employed about forty men. The salt plant was producing four hundred barrels of salt each day, and the ice plant was producing fifty tons of ice each day.[89]

As the new Carey Salt Company grew, so did the county. After a fire and because the county had outgrown its small courthouse across the street from Carey Salt, a new Reno County Courthouse was constructed and completed

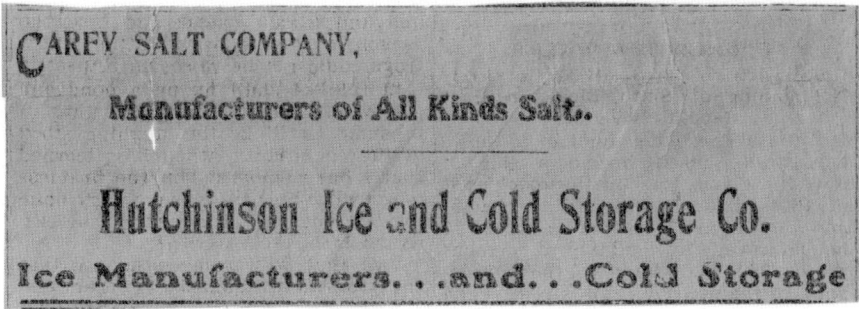

CAREY SALT COMPANY,

Manufacturers of All Kinds Salt.

Hutchinson Ice and Cold Storage Co.

Ice Manufacturers...and...Cold Storage

Emerson ran very simple advertisements in newspapers in the early years of the ice and salt companies. *Reno County Museum Collection.*

right next door to the then fledgling Carey Salt Company at the southeast corner of Avenue B and Main. The courthouse was built of brick and limestone and was a grand style with a soaring square dome. The location of this courthouse would later play a haunting role in Emerson's future.[90]

In 1903, things were moving along well for the small independent Carey Salt Company. Emerson's goal was to sell one-third of the salt coming out of Hutchinson. Emerson made major additions to the facility this year, including drilling another well using company employees as labor this time, rather than contracting the work out. This increased the company's worth to $100,000. The company's expansion and Emerson's goal would have put a dent in the sales of the powerful salt trust. These two facts forced the trust to pay attention once more to the small independent salt company. The salt trust had a reputation of assimilating or eliminating small salt companies in Hutchinson by using railroad tariffs to get better freight rates. Railroads coming into Hutchinson at the time were the Missouri Pacific; the Rock Island; the Atchison, Topeka and Santa Fe; and the Hutchinson and Arkansas River Railroad. These railroads combined to place tariffs on freight. However, the Hutchinson and Arkansas River Railroad, which had no rolling stock and only two thousand feet of rail, was owned by Joy Morton's Hutchinson-Kansas Salt Company. Emerson commented about Morton and his Hutchinson and Arkansas River Railroad, "He organized a railroad and called it the Hutchinson and Arkansas River Railroad. It started nowhere and ended at the same place. He had no engines, cars or other equipment."[91] Despite this fact, the Hutchinson-Kansas Salt Company trust was rebated moneys from tariffs paid for by the independent salt companies. The Hutchinson and Arkansas River Railroad was allegedly set up by

By 1903, it's clear that Emerson's salt industry now has top billing over his hide, coal and ice companies at 226 South Main. *Conard-Harmon Collection.*

Morton to connect Hutchinson to Kechi, Kansas, where the Chicago, Rock Island and Pacific Lines were located. But in reality, as Emerson discovered, it really only had a switch line. And so, a rebate was demanded for freight traveling from Hutchinson to the Missouri River of 25 percent but not more than fifty cents a ton.[92]

Emerson and the other independent salt producers could not compete with the rebates that Morton received via the fake railroad. Their salt sales dwindled. Finally, the independents caught the attention of the Interstate Commerce Commission, which began to investigate this suspicious practice. It was in direct violation of the 1903 Elkins Act, which outlawed the payments of rebates to preferred customers. The commerce commission sent a Mr. C.A. Prouty to Hutchinson to hear testimony from the independent salt producers. Prouty discovered that, indeed, a rebate was being paid to the Hutchinson and Arkansas River Railroad. Prouty also discovered that all the officers of the River Railroad were managers of the salt trust. Finally,

Joy Morton was called to testify. Under Prouty's sharp questioning, Morton was forced to disclose that "he supposed the proceeds of his salt company had gone into his right hand pocket and the money earned by the division of freight rates had gone into his left hand pocket." Prouty reported his findings to the Interstate Commerce Commission, which ruled that the Hutchinson and Arkansas River Railroad was set up by the salt trust to capture rebates in direct violation of the Elkins Act.[93]

Having resolved the freight rebate issue successfully in his favor, Emerson breathed a bit easier and turned to other pursuits; his support of Charles Winchester increased. Winchester sold his meat market in 1903 and established the Winchester Packing Company at 16 West Avenue F. The packing company also comprised the Kansas Hide Company. It did not come as a surprise when Charles's son Stanley Allen married Emerson's sister Edith that same year. By 1907, the Winchester Packing Company was earning $150,000 worth of business.[94] The Winchester Packing Company utilized the space of the Hutchinson Ice and Cold Storage Plant.[95]

Hutchinson wasn't the only location where Emerson was involved in the ice industry. Perhaps to help a friend get started in the ice business, Emerson, J.G. Puterbaugh, George Coble and G.W. Huff started the Pueblo Ice and Coal Company in Pueblo, Colorado, which was incorporated in 1904.[96] Using $50,000 in capital, Emerson built a production facility that produced twenty tons of ice per day. Emerson was president and Huff was the manager. In comparison, the Hutchinson location was producing forty-five to fifty tons of ice per day. At about this same time, Emerson expanded the cold storage facility in Hutchinson. The new addition to the Hutchinson Ice and Cold Storage Company was open in September 1904, just in time for the fall apple season. The new warehouse could hold fifteen thousand barrels of apples.[97] The cold storage facility in Hutchinson also held butter and poultry.

Emerson was always looking to expand his existing business interests, and this was true with his new salt empire as well. Emerson somehow received word that the S.Q. Richardson family of Grand Saline, Texas, was selling their salt company, known as the Richardson Salt Works. S.Q. passed away in 1900, and the family had tried to keep the company operating after his death. Emerson and J. Kirk, his brother-in-law, started the Grand Saline Salt Company in 1904 as a front to purchase the Richardson holdings. With Emerson as president, they soon hired and partnered with T.S. McGrain to manage the operation. McGrain expanded the operation to a capacity of 750 barrels of salt a day.[98]

As early as 1904, there were some rumblings of Emerson's toying with entering politics. An editorial piece in the local *Saturday Bee* newspaper, titled "Idle Thoughts of a Boy," expressed the writer's displeasure at the thought of Emerson entering the world of politics: "He was sorry that some of Emerson Carey's friends were trying to spoil the good business man by making him a candidate for legislature. There you are. It needs a good business man to sit on the city council, but do not spoil a business man by sending him to the legislature."[99] The editorial comment worked on Emerson for a short time, but it wouldn't be long before the lure of the legislature was too strong for the ever-expanding and ever-learning powerhouse that Emerson had become.

He was already entrenched in politics of a different kind when, having already been a member of the Masons for some time, in 1904, Emerson became a thirty-second-degree Mason. He was a member of the Blue Lodge and Commandery of Hutchinson and a member of the Consistory of Wichita. Additionally, Emerson was a member of the Hutchinson Lodge of the Ancient Order of the United Workmen, Knights Templar, Isis Temple of the Mystic Shrine at Salina and the Knights and Ladies of Security.[100]

Other more local opportunities, however, began to catch Emerson's eye during the early 1900s as well. In 1904, J.J. Burns was given a franchise to establish Hutchinson's first electric streetcar line.[101] However, Burns failed to come through, so in 1905, the Hutchinson Commercial Club took steps to fulfill the franchise. The goal was to raise $32,400, of which Emerson donated $2,000 and his employees raised $1,050. The Commercial Club then bought the horse-drawn streetcar line. Emerson, Charles M. Williams and K.E. Sentney paid $8,000 to Mr. Bigger, who owned the old horse-drawn trolley. The city then granted the franchise for the electric streetcar line to them on a fifty-year basis. The Commercial Club elected Emerson the interim president of the Hutchinson Street Railway Company. Emerson became president, Williams was vice president, A.W. Smith served as secretary, Sentney was treasurer and C.H. McBurney served on the board as well. At the time, it traversed about five miles through Hutchinson with about sixteen horsecars. Emerson and the other officers were eventually charged with raising as near to $100,000 as possible to make the electric streetcar line a reality.[102]

Almost simultaneously with Emerson's foray into the world of transportation, Emerson and the same group of partners, along with the Hutchinson Commercial Club, began the People's Water, Light, and Power Company. Emerson was already producing power at the ice plant,

A 1904 certificate naming Emerson as a thirty-second-degree Master in the Ancient and Accepted Scottish Rite. *Reno County Museum Collection.*

so forming the power company was a natural fit. People's would eventually supply electrical power for the trolley, for Emerson's interests on South Main Street and possibly for his neighbors as well. This created great problems for Emerson and his group because the existing Water, Light, and Gas Company claimed it had been given exclusive rights to the franchise to furnish power to Hutchinson. The complaint resulted in litigation in which the Water, Light, and Gas Company sued the City of Hutchinson for franchise rights.[103] The outcome of the litigation was that Emerson and the Commercial Club were validated in their right to operate the new People's Water, Light, and Power Company.

Although Emerson won the battle against the competing power company, sadly, his father, Samuel, lost his fight on March 9, 1905, when his roving, adventurous life came at last to an end. He was buried in Eastside Cemetery alongside his wife, Nancy Jane Bundy Carey, in Hutchinson, Kansas.[104]

Emerson became heavily involved with the Kansas Ice Men's Association as early as 1904. Emerson spoke at the 1905 Ice Men's Association meeting, and a few segments of his speech were quoted in the April issue of the *Ice*

The offices at 327 North Main housed Emerson's People's Water, Power, and Light and the Hutchinson Inter-Urban Railway Companies, circa 1909. *Conard-Harmon Collection.*

and Refrigeration Journal from that year. This quote gave a small glimpse into Emerson's sense of humor:

> *A great many of us practical icemen know about as much about how an ice plant is put together as the little girl that went to Sunday school for the first time. Her teacher wanted to enlighten her about the various functions of the body. She told her that her little ears were made to hear with and her eyes were made to see with; that her nose was made to smell with and her feet were made to run with. She immediately began to cry and the teacher said: "What is the matter?" She said, "I am put together wrong. My nose runs and my feet smell."*

In that same journal, Emerson discussed his refrigeration plant, saying that it handled twenty thousand barrels of apples and was 136,000 cubic feet with a north front that opened out to get ventilation. He described the building as having an "insulated trapdoor about two feet square. When the temperature on the outside gets to 30 degrees, we open the doors to get ventilation." Emerson informed the audience that he had a salt plant in Texas. He also advised the audience about how to sell ice at a profit, saying that the ice man "must learn that you can catch more flies with molasses than you can with vinegar." A revealing quote into Emerson's own self-perception can also be found in his speech as printed in the 1905 *Ice and Refrigeration Journal*: "I have been trying to figure out why I was called on to make a speech, as I was never regarded as a speaker. I might be termed what you would call a buttinsky."[105]

In early 1905, Emerson struck a deal with the Swift Packing Company to construct a building complete with refrigeration supplied by Emerson's ice plant. Henry Shears was chosen as the building contractor for this new poultry packinghouse at Avenue E and Main. Only a couple of doors away, the area of Avenue C and Main Street held a lot of Emerson's businesses and buildings. The Carey Salt Company was here, along with the Carey Ice plant. Winchester Packing was nearby, and one of Emerson's large cold storage facilities for apples was at Avenue E and Washington. This group of Emerson's buildings formed a sort of city where Emerson supplied water, electrical power and refrigeration to his buildings. This little "Carey" city was given the name "Careyville" by the locals—a name that must have put a smile on Emerson's face.[106]

Another insight into Emerson's personality and others' opinion about him came during a brief disagreement Emerson had with the city council during 1905. In December, the city wanted to pave the street in front of Emerson's buildings; Emerson argued against this and moved to stop the city. At the same time, he requested permission to use the sidewalk alongside his buildings on East Avenue C to build a platform to be able to load and unload rail cars on the Missouri Pacific switching line. The city did pass an ordinance allowing

The Swift Packing Company cold storage business, at Avenue E and Main, turned to Emerson for construction of its new refrigeration building in Hutchinson. *Hutchinson/Reno Chamber of Commerce Collection.*

Emerson's sprawling empire along Avenue C and Main about 1908 was known at the time as "Careyville." *Reno County Museum Collection.*

Battling the powerful salt trust, Emerson's Carey Salt aligned with the smaller independent salt companies, such as Barton Salt, shown here in an early photograph. *Reno County Museum Collection.*

him to do this, with the condition that he had to remove the platforms at any given time requested by the city with thirty days' written notice. Some on the council had argued against giving him permission; they wanted to punish him for arguing against paving the street. Others prevailed, saying that the platforms would encourage further business activity, and thus more taxable property would be created, which would all be good for the city. The council apologized to Emerson over the spat, admitting that "Mr. Carey...is a pretty 'good sort of guy,' after all." Emerson replied that he "had no sore spots," and to prove it, he sent up a box of cigars to the council members. "Thereupon the city administrators smoked the cigars of peace, about two apiece."[107]

Emerson's speech at the Western Ice Manufacturers' Association eighth annual meeting in 1906 provided further insight into his personality and perspectives about the ice industry and the business world as a whole. He stated, "There is no doubt about the scripture admonition that 'Brethren should dwell together in unity.' as applied to all manner of business as conducted today." He also asserted, "In my opinion, the ice man is the worst abused man in the country, doubtless for the reason that by the nature of things his business is often a monopoly....The ice man really is the 'salt of the earth.'" In 1907, Emerson was elected president of the association at its ninth annual meeting held in Kansas City, Missouri, in February. It's a testimony to his charisma, capability and effectiveness that Emerson was

Local road builders Shears & Sons owned stock in the Hutchinson Inter-Urban Railway Company in 1913. *Reno County Museum Collection.*

Horse-drawn wagons vie for space with the electric streetcars on Main Street. *Reno County Museum Collection.*

The 1906 opening of the Hutchinson Inter-Urban was met with much fanfare at Sherman and Main Streets. *Conard-Harmon Collection.*

elected president, even though he himself had been accused by his peers of being in an ice trust during 1906.[108]

In January 1906, a charter was granted, and the Hutchinson Street Railway Company became the Hutchinson Inter-Urban Railway Company. The board of directors included Emerson Carey, T.J. Templer, K.E. Sentney, E.T. Guymon, J.A. Fontron, J.P. Shunk, C.M. Williams, J.S. George, W.Y. Morgan, A.W. Smith and L.A. Bunker. The capital stock in the company was $100,000. It was planned for cars to traverse seven miles of the city, with connections to other rail lines going to the nearby locations of Haven, Brandy Lake, Nickerson, Sterling and Huntsville.[109]

CHAPTER 5

SODA ASH IS WHERE IT'S AT

1906–1910

Emerson's fourth and last child, Emerson Carey Jr., was born in 1906.[110] Having three boys and the birth of a fourth would have been enough to keep the average family busy, but it wasn't enough for Emerson. He directed his interests in the flagging soda ash business that was sparking the imaginations of wealthy and powerful investors in Hutchinson. Soda ash (anhydrous sodium carbonate) was used to make types of glass and was also used in soaps and detergents. Soda ash was made using the then well-known Solvay process. In this process, three basic chemicals are used to produce soda ash: brine (salt and water), limestone and ammonia.[111]

In 1906, a local man, John Parker, became aware of the idea that salt brine was one of the main ingredients in soda ash. Hutchinson, with its immense salt deposits running beneath it and large concentration of salt companies, seemed to be a prime location for this new business. Dr. S.H. Colladay became intrigued with the idea and brought in John Faulkner, an English chemical engineer, to explore this enticing business opportunity. Faulkner proposed that if Hutchinson could raise $50,000, he would raise the remainder of the $450,000 he estimated it would take to build the soda ash plant. He was successful in raising $250,000 by selling stock in Hutchinson, Halstead, McPherson and other nearby cities. However, Emerson had his doubts about Faulkner's success and so invested only $1,000 in the company. While Faulkner worked out the science and finances of this new venture, a group of businessmen formed with Colladay as president, Charles N. Sentney as secretary, James B. MacClay as treasurer and Emerson Carey

This 1908 photograph of the Kansas Chemical Manufacturing Company represents the operation in its infancy. *Reno County Museum Collection.*

and Charles M. Williams as general members of the board of directors. Thus, the Hutchinson Chemical and Alkali Company, also known as the Kansas Chemical Manufacturing Company, was on the verge of opening for business.

Although Faulkner had raised a good amount of capital, it wasn't enough to cover equipment, construction and operating costs. Bonds were issued at sixty cents on the dollar, and investors Sentney, Mr. Steele, Mr. Bunker, Mr. McNair and Mr. Peet purchased these in amounts varying from $10,000 to $25,000. Still wary of the operation, Emerson purchased only $4,000 of the bonds. Even with the influx of this additional financing, the plant performed poorly, with low-quality products, unreliable equipment and small output. Emerson increased his involvement in the finances of the company at this time, demanding financial and status reports. Finally, Dr. Colladay resigned as president and urged Emerson to take his place. Although Emerson had no faith in the company and was very hesitant, he eventually relented and became president. Consulting experienced men in related chemical and manufacturing fields, Emerson quickly discovered that the purchased equipment was not large enough to be able to produce the projected 120 tons of soda ash daily. At the most, the company made one-third of that. The company was losing $300 each day and soon began to lose $500 per

Construction of an expansion to the Kansas Chemical Manufacturing Company. *Reno County Museum Collection.*

day. Emerson twice recommended that the plant be closed; however, in the end, he structured a reorganization of the company and raised the necessary $110,000 to make the plant at least operable.[112]

Evidently, the city of Hutchinson and investors still had incredibly high hopes for this new enterprise, or the marketing department of the company was very good, as evidenced by the following blurb that appeared in the promotional booklet *The Salt City Industrial Review and Commercial Booklet of Hutchinson*: "The Kansas Chemical Manufacturing Corporation which recently was re-organized with increased capital is located here but a few rods outside the city limits. While this concern, which will manufacture soda ash, still has to reach the goal of successful enterprise, its future is assured owing to the many ways in which soda ash can be utilized this will mean that millions of tons of the product will be shipped from Hutchinson yearly within a short time."[113] While the city of Hutchinson boasted about this new business, it would be several more years before Emerson found a solution to the soda ash problem.

In 1908, Emerson focused his attention on Anthony, Kansas, where he erected a new ice plant with a twenty-five-ton ice-making capacity. This was another case where Emerson probably began this company to help out a friend and then very quickly reduced his presence within the company.[114] The plant equipment was manufactured by the Milwaukee, Wisconsin firm of Vilter Manufacturing Company. As Emerson was highly respected in the ice

The city of Hutchinson thought the prospects looked good for the newly constructed Kansas Chemical Manufacturing Corporation. *Reno County Museum Collection.*

and refrigeration field, the Western Ice Manufacturers' Association elected him as an official delegate that year to the First International Congress of Refrigerating Industries. At the Congress, Emerson gave a speech titled "The Mistakes of the Ice Man." Emerson noted in his speech that one of the greatest mistakes an ice man could make was "to not get a fair price for his products." Another warning Emerson gave to the delegates was, "I think it is a great mistake not to know every detail of your business from the coal pile to the bank account." Other advice he dished out was that the selling department was crucial to any business and that competition should "visit each other and exchange views and ideas…to sell the most ice at reasonable prices" (this last being a very progressive viewpoint at the time for someone so competitive, but also strikingly similar to the tactics used by the big trusts of the era). And finally, Emerson told the crowd, "I think one of the greatest mistakes the ice man makes is not to keep cool—always keep a piece of ice in your hat."[115]

Although Emerson's father, Samuel, had thrown his hat in the political ring a couple of times while he was alive, politics was one place Emerson had yet to test the waters. However, with his usual fearless manner, Emerson ran for the state senate in 1908 on the Republican ticket. His campaign was successful, and in November, he was elected the state senator of the Thirty-Sixth Kansas State Senatorial District, representing Reno, Pratt and Kingman Counties.[116] This new venture was to last through two terms and became a fruitful and robust experience for Emerson.

With his four young sons, thriving businesses and now a senatorial seat under his belt, it's hard to believe that Emerson had any time for rest and relaxation. However, perhaps that's exactly why Emerson was such an avid golfer—the need to get away from his business interests combined with his

Emerson Carey. *Reno County Museum Collection.*

fierce competitiveness. Golf must have been a natural outlet for him. He played in some of the state's very first golf tournaments. Left-handed and tall, Emerson must have seemed quite intimidating on the course. Local golf champ Dayul Donaldson remembered playing with Emerson: "He didn't hit a very long ball....Yes, he was a good golfer, and he liked to play golf, and he liked to see it done right. If you could do it right, he wanted it done that way. He was an excellent golfer." Margaret Waddles Hipple (female state golf champion for four straight years from 1926 to 1929) stated, "I have never known a man who loved to play golf so much as Emerson Carey."[117] Patty Carey (married to Emerson's grandson Howard "Jake" Carey) later remarked, "At age sixty-two [Emerson's] game of golf was the envy of men half his age. In his library were dozens of trophies which he had won in tournaments all over the country. He shot an average eighteen-hole course in less than seventy-five."[118]

As an extension of his love for golf and a need to cement his status in the community, Emerson was very passionate about establishing a new country club in Hutchinson. He served on the promotional committee for the club from the very beginning. Emerson was elected as the first director and the first president of the Hutchinson Country Club in 1908.[119] This first country club, completed while he was president, was located on the east side of Hutchinson, very near the Kansas Chemical Manufacturing Company, on North Halsted Street.[120]

In July 1908, Emerson's fierce appetite for golf was again shown as he and several friends—Reverend Paul Talbot, S.F. Hutton, J.S. George, Grant Chamberland and Claude Adams—went to Wichita to attend the state golf championship. The golf tournament was, of course, one reason he attended; but another, perhaps more important, reason may have been a planned meeting to form a Kansas golf association. No such association had existed in Kansas until this time. Reverend Talbot was elected the first president of the golf association that year.[121]

Emerson's competitive nature and drive to be first may have influenced his choice of automobiles as well. In 1908, Emerson bought a White Steamer. It was the first Steamer in Hutchinson—a luxurious car owned by the richest of people. President Teddy Roosevelt had one in his White House, although he never rode in it. President Taft also owned a Steamer and is known as the first president to fully embrace the automobile. It is fitting that Emerson would be drawn to a steam-powered auto, as most of his industries relied on steam as a power source. Emerson would be very familiar with the power of steam. Even though he enjoyed having two automobiles and loved his Steamer, that didn't keep it from blowing up. On September 22 that year, Emerson left the gas jet on while the safety valve was off. The hood blew off and the front windshield was busted, but no one was injured.[122]

While Emerson was getting his feet wet in the senate, working out the kinks of the soda ash plant and directing his coal, ice and salt companies—and playing golf—the stirrings of yet another new company were on the horizon in 1908. Eastern investors recognized the fact that there was a market for the massive amounts of wheat straw byproducts left over from all the wheat growers in the area. The straw could be turned into pulp and eventually formed into a stiff board used as wallboard in construction. So, convinced of the success of a potential wallboard company, the investors came to Hutchinson and purchased land to be the site for a future manufacturing company. James L. Carey, of Chicago, Illinois, was chosen as architect and engineer to design the plant, and so the Western Strawboard Company was established. The first machine began operating in 1909 with the capability of producing thirty to thirty-five tons of wallboard per day. The board of directors consisted of J.S. Cline, president of Fleischer Paper Box Company of Chicago; A.M. Sheperd, president of the Vincennes Paper Company of Vincennes, Indiana; S.A.D. Whipple, manufacturer of Filler Machinery of Portland, Indiana; W.H. Underwood, president of the Underwood & Viles Cold Storage Company of Hutchinson, Kansas; William G. Fairchild, Hutchinson attorney; Lewis H. Falley, manager of the Western Straw

A large stockpile of straw awaits processing outside the Western Straw Products Company. *Reno County Museum Collection.*

Products Company; and Edward S. Shepherd, who was the superintendent of the company. Soon the strawboard production capacity was up to fifty tons per day. However, the original investors were only interested in getting rich quick, heavily promoting the sale of stock and selling lots to the employees. Soon, things turned rocky and disappointed stockholders were dishing out additional funds to support the struggling business.[123] It wouldn't be long before Emerson once again became a "buttinsky" and stepped in to rescue this sinking venture.

While the strawboard company struggled, in 1909 Emerson's salt and other interests were going like gangbusters. Emerson began to erect a new, fireproof salt plant, made of steel and cement, east of the city limits, and by June 1910, the new plant opened. Emerson installed grainer pans here as well, but what made the East Plant the most modern and unique in the industry was the Lillie "quadruple effect" vacuum pans that Emerson installed. The vacuum pan system heated the salt brine in large tanks called "effects." With a quadruple system, Emerson now had four tanks that worked together to evaporate the brine. A vacuum created inside the tank lowered the boiling

Early production of paper products at the Western Straw Products Company utilized only waste from the wheat industry. *Reno County Museum Collection.*

point of the brine, the salt dropped out and was removed and the steam was filtered into the next "effect" or tank. The steam could then be reused, with each effect requiring a lower boiling point than the last one. One old-style grainer pan used one pound of steam to make one pound of salt. With four vacuum pans, the same one pound of steam could make four pounds of salt. The new system was by far more efficient.[124]

It had long been held a Carey Salt Company legend that when building the new east Carey Salt plant, Emerson had ordered the smokestack to be 106 feet tall. The story goes that Emerson told the designers to make the smokestack that height because he knew that Morton Salt's smokestack was 100 feet tall. He is rumored to have said, "Morton's stands 100 feet in Hutchinson, but Carey's stands taller."[125]

The building of the "East Plant," as it was known in the Carey Salt Company, and the use of the new quadruple pan system invoked the outrage of the salt trust, i.e., Joy Morton. Emerson learned that Morton had told Houston Whiteside, a prominent local judge, and Mrs. Whiteside, his wife, that "I will not tolerate the operation of that plant. I am sorry they are putting in the Lillie Vacuum system because I expect to finally own the plant and do not like the Lillie Vacuum." In a later business trip to Chicago,

Opened in 1910, the East Plant of the Carey Salt Company was the most modern of its kind at the time. *Reno County Museum Collection.*

Adding the Lillie vacuum system put Emerson Carey's salt company on the cutting edge of modern salt-producing operations in 1909. *Reno County Museum Collection.*

The addition of the Lillie quadruple effect vacuum system made Emerson's salt evaporation plant one of the most modern in the world. *Reno County Museum Collection.*

Emerson stopped into Morton's office to talk with him about salt prices. During the meeting, Morton told Emerson that there was "plenty of salt making capacity in the [Kansas] field and Emerson had no right to increase his output." Emerson told Morton he would contact him when the plant was in operation. Emerson did call Morton after the plant was in operation to

The long white buildings held grainer pans that were originally used to dry salt. The tallest building housed the Lillie quadruple effect vacuum system. *Reno County Museum Collection.*

again attempt to discuss prices and tonnage. Morton asked Emerson what tonnage he thought he was entitled to. Emerson's response probably made Morton's jaw hit the floor, as he told him, "One third of the Kansas field." Morton replied, "It would cost you more money to prove that than it cost to build the plant."[126]

Emerson knew that Morton's threat was hollow because he had survived the same threat by Frank Vincent and the salt trust when he first entered the salt circus. With the new East Plant about to go into operation, Emerson's visions of resourcefulness and self-reliance would continue to prove his stability.

The year 1909 was a good one for ice and the cold storage business. Emerson's cold companies had another name change this year to the Carey Ice and Cold Storage Company, reflecting a subtle change focusing now on the Carey name recognition rather than Hutchinson. The ice and storage business had really grown in the last three years. Back in 1906, an addition had been made to the plant that drew it closer to several of the rail lines: the Chicago, Rock Island and Pacific Railway Companies. This further linked Emerson's company to supplying ice for cooling down the railway cars. In 1908, the cold storage capacity was increased, and triple sets of machinery were installed for redundancy to control temperatures in the storage plant in case of any breakdowns and failures.[127]

Sometime between 1908 and 1910, Emerson purchased a Winton auto. Wintons were known as being some of the first autos made in the United States. The photo of the Winton in front of Emerson's home at 821 North Main shows how much pride Emerson took in his autos. The interesting thing about this particular Winton and what makes it difficult to date is that it has the front fenders of a 1910 model but the back fenders of a 1908 model. This probably meant it was an in-between model that the company started building in the 1910s but still used leftover 1908 parts to complete. Emerson would surely have been proud of the fact that his custom Winton may have been one of a kind.[128]

In early 1909, Emerson became involved in building a $35,000 packing plant at the corner of Avenue C and Walnut. Other investors in this business were J.P. Harsha, W.Y. Morgan and K.E. Sentney. The building was planned to be an L-shaped, three-story multipurpose building to serve as a local branch of the United States Packing Company. It was designed to hold as many as eighteen thousand chickens, with the first floor housing offices, cold storage rooms and butter packing rooms. The second floor was to be the picking room with some feeding rooms, while the third floor was to house the majority of the feeding stations for the chickens. This new business, the Emerson, Marlow Produce Company, focused on fattening young chickens for market. However, on November 11, 1909, the structure caught fire, and at least eleven thousand chickens were lost in the fire along with the building, for a total loss of about $50,000. The fire was so intense that it took nearly a week to put it out.[129]

Emerson was involved more intimately with another fire in 1909. While the legislature was in session, Emerson was staying at the Copeland Hotel in Topeka. The hotel was often called "The County Copeland" and was known as a gathering place for Republican politicians. At 4:00 a.m. on January 15, the hotel caught fire. Emerson and other guests were startled out of their warm beds and forced to evacuate in their pajamas by jumping out of windows. All of their clothing was lost in the fire, and Emerson and his colleagues had to make a trip to a clothing store barefoot and wearing only their nightclothes. Emerson, minus his clothing, escaped unharmed, but the hotel was a total loss.[130]

After the produce company fire and the hotel fire, Emerson was surely on guard to not get burned again, but he was on fire in a good way in 1909 with his senatorial efforts. Emerson had a long history of fighting the freight industry, and this culminated in his helping to secure passage of a freight rate limitation bill.[131] It's sure that he felt victorious at the passage of this

Anna May and Emerson lived in the home at 821 North Main about 1915. *Conard-Harmon Collection.*

Emerson and Anna May sit on the porch at 821 North Main, admiring their luxury Winton car, about 1910. *Conard-Harmon Collection.*

The top floor of the Emerson, Marlow Produce Company building is shown with its windows open, a necessity for ventilation when full of chickens. *Reno County Museum Collection.*

bill after his many fights with Joy Morton and the railroads. Emerson also helped save a bill granting state aid to cities for the construction of armories. However, he fought unsuccessfully to get the senate bill (the bill dearest to his heart) to officially establish the state fair in Hutchinson passed through the House of Representatives. Never one to give in, Emerson was to persist with this battle for years to come.

Things weren't all pompous and straight-laced in these early days in the senate. Emerson played a central role in a comical affair during 1909. Apparently, it came about that Senator John Overfield, representing Montgomery County, Kansas, thought the color of the doorkeeper's beard was unpleasant. Overfield mentioned this to Emerson, who spread the comment throughout the senate. At Emerson's suggestion, Senator Brady of Douglas County introduced the following resolution: "Whereas Senator Overfield has objected to the color of the whiskers of the man who stands at the door of the entrance of the senate, therefore be it resolved, that the afore-designated employee be instructed to change the color of his beard so as to satisfy the taste of the senator from Montgomery." Emerson heartily signed off on the light-hearted resolution.[132]

THE KANSAS STATE FAIR---HUTCHINSON
The Great Agricultural and Live Stock Event of the Southwest.
B-9 TALBOTT-ENO CO., DES MOINES SEPTEMBER 11 TO 17, 1909, INCLUSIVE.

In 1909, Emerson was still battling the Topeka senators for the right to name Hutchinson as the official site of the Kansas State Fair. *Reno County Museum Collection.*

Back at the salt company, salt production capacity in 1910 was 2,200 barrels daily. But because of the price war that had begun the year before between Morton and Emerson, production lagged behind sales, with Emerson's Carey Salt Company falling two hundred cars behind in shipments and Morton Salt falling four hundred cars behind. Morton then approached Emerson with the idea that they raise the price of salt to slow down demand. Gradually, the price rose back to eighty-five cents per barrel. With this collaborative effort to raise salt prices, the predictions that the Chicago steel man had given Emerson about the salt trust were completely fulfilled.[133]

In fact, the salt company was so successful that on June 17, 1910, Emerson created a charter for the Hutchinson Salt Company to become a subsidiary under the Carey Salt Company. Hutchinson Salt was to become the sales force unit for Carey Salt, with one of its very first salesmen, R.G. Streeter, as its first secretary. Streeter had just graduated as a stenographer from the Salt City Business College (aptly named to reflect the impact that the salt industry had on Hutchinson) and was the driving force behind a change in advertising methods that was to take place much later in the Carey Salt

A 1910 stock certificate for five shares in the Western Straw Products Company. *Reno County Museum Collection.*

Company. The Carey Ice and Cold Storage Company was producing eighty-five tons of ice each day in 1910 with three refrigeration units—two at seventy-five tons and one at forty tons. Emerson's Cold Storage Company consisted of half a million cubic feet of space and could now handle 100,000 barrels of produce consisting of flour, apples, poultry and butter.[134]

Emerson's world had changed immensely from twenty-six years earlier with the humble beginnings of his career running mule teams in Hale's coal business. It must have seemed like the end of an era when, in 1910, Emerson closed the Carey Coal Company.[135]

CHAPTER 6

THE VERY FAIR SENATOR

1911–1916

E merson turned his efforts to his ice interests at this time as he became the president of the Kansas Ice Men's Association in 1911. Not satisfied with only ice, soda ash, fibre products and salt, there were reports that Emerson was also interested in a school desk factory and a soap factory, although there's no evidence of Emerson being involved in the establishment of those two businesses during this time.[136]

With industry exploding and the city continuing to grow, in 1911, Emerson pushed for legislation that would make his beloved city of Hutchinson a first-class city. He also resisted increases in municipal levies for water and electrical service. He was successful in both these endeavors. Kansas's first workmen's compensation act was enacted in 1911, and Emerson made sure to secure the inclusion of salt workers within this act. However, one of the most notable efforts that Emerson fought for in the senate was his drive to secure that the state fair of Kansas be located in Hutchinson. Forever the city backer, Emerson recognized early on what a boon the fair could be to whatever city possessed it. Emerson wasn't the only one to recognize the potential of securing the location for the state fair. As early as 1871, Topeka hosted the first state fair. The Kansas State Fair Association was formed in 1881 in Topeka, where a total of eighty acres was designated for the fair. Other cities had also hosted their own "state fairs" before this, but there was no official, permanent home for the "Kansas State Fair." Likewise, Hutchinson had been holding its own fair, organized by the Reno County Agricultural Society, as early as 1873, and in 1875, it became the First

Old-fashioned wagons met modern technology at the Carey Ice Company at 216 South Main around 1912. *Conard-Harmon Collection.*

Annual Reno County Fair. Once the association in Topeka was formed, the state fair was held in Topeka on the eighty acres from 1881 to 1883 and from 1893 to 1896, and in 1902, the fair began to be held there annually. This was due to the Kansas State Fair Association entering a ten-year agreement to hold the fair there. Unfortunately for Emerson in 1911, there was an unfriendly House of Representatives in Topeka, and in this case, Emerson's efforts were thwarted.[137] He may have lost the match again this year, but he certainly hadn't been thrown out of the ring for good.

Back home in Hutchinson in 1908, Emerson offered plots of his land on the south bank of the Arkansas River to the City of Hutchinson to use as parkland; however, he continued to purchase land in that area along the river throughout '08 and '09. By 1911, the park area, part of Riverside Park, had become a lovely recreation area with stone gates, rustic seats, swings and a broad boulevard ready for traffic.[138]

A busy 1911 came to a close, and 1912 opened with a vengeance. Early January 1912 was a particularly brutal time, with lows in the zero range and winds at gale force from the north. So, Emerson, always a patron of the poor, wrote a letter to Captain Seeds of the Salvation Army. In the letter, Emerson promised to donate forty thousand pounds of coal, the contents of an entire rail car. The letter stated that Emerson wished to help forty needy families with one-thousand-pound lots of coal being distributed to each. Emerson did not end it there. He also told Captain Seeds that anyone with a wagon and a letter from Captain Seeds could go to his plant and they would be given an equal allotment. After discovering that Captain Seeds's own daughter was in need, Emerson asked the *Gazette*, a local newspaper, to report on the Seeds family's need. Katie Seeds was stricken with tuberculosis. Her doctor had told Captain Seeds that her only hope was to go to Arizona, where the warm, dry climate would help her recovery. The *Gazette* suggested to its readers that aid was needed for the Seeds family. The following is an early list of donors at that time, with Emerson's name and larger donation prominently listed at the top:

> *Emerson Carey*.................$25.00
> *The Gazette*........................5.00
> *Rev. Toothacker*...................2.50
> *John Bertche*........................1.00
> *Cash*..............................12.50
> *Cash*................................3.00

Later in the month, Emerson discovered that "negroes" were not given coal or were too proud to ask. According to C.O. Smith, a leading member of the black community, "Mr. Carey was a real benefactor during the recent cold spell." Smith was in charge of distributing twenty tons of the coal to poor members of the black community.[139]

It was at this point that Emerson admitted that he and the board of the Kansas Chemical Manufacturing Company were out of their element. He contacted the Solvay Process Company to offer it the opportunity to buy out the soda ash stock. The Solvay Process Company, with locations in Syracuse, New York, and Detroit, Michigan, specialized in making soda ash from salt brine and limestone. By this time, Emerson had invested $50,000 to keep the plant operating. After many visits, in 1912, Emerson and the Solvay Process Company reached an agreement in the amount of $600,000 for the purchase of the stock. Emerson had achieved his goal of minimizing loss for the stockholders and board members in what could have been ultimate failure. Even after the sale, Emerson remained on as vice president of the company.[140]

During the World War I era, the Solvay Process Company employed enough men to field its own baseball team. *Reno County Museum Collection.*

Having resolved the issues of the soda ash company, in 1912, Emerson, with the help of his son Howard, started to look at the possibility of building a rock salt mine in Hutchinson.[141] The market for rock salt was great, both in using it to ice down rail cars to keep them cool as they traveled across the country and also in agriculture as a feed supplement for livestock.

Emerson's son Howard Carey.
Reno County Museum Collection.

Emerson and Howard must have realized that mining rock salt was cheaper to produce than evaporating salt from brine and would be acceptable in such uses. Even though the rock salt mine was just an idea at this point, Emerson was still innovating and pushing the limits of his companies. For several years, his was the only company compressing the salt into a solid block to be used by cattle, goats, sheep and other stock. Emerson even had an extensive herd of test cattle near the salt plant to be able to test these new "Carey-ized" block salt stock products.[142]

On the evening of June 27, 1912, a peculiar thing happened that showed the overwhelming love and care the people of Hutchinson had for Emerson. This night, somehow a mule tied to a power pole guy line became electrocuted at the Carey Ice Plant. The news got out that Emerson had been electrocuted while inspecting machinery at the ice plant. The tragic rumor of Emerson's electrocution spread through Hutchinson like the wind for which Kansas is known. Soon the phones at the *Hutchinson News* began to ring off the desks and walls. The *News* reporters rushed to verify the story by calling around to all of Emerson's usual hangouts. Finally, they tracked Emerson down to the country club where he was playing golf with family. Upon hearing the news of his demise, he quickly called first his family and then his businesses to dispel the story and calm fears. It was never learned exactly how the mule was electrified. No power could be measured on the guy line, which was firmly grounded into the soil. However, Walter Grundy of the United Water, Gas, and Electric Company stated that mules were very susceptible to electrical currents and had died from exposure to stray ground currents.[143]

False rumors of his death aside, a very-much-alive Emerson was elected president of the Sterling Coal Mining Company in Featherstone, Oklahoma, in 1912. Also, local parks continued to be foremost on his mind in 1912, as Emerson attempted to secure a bond issue that would establish a city park system. Although he was not successful in obtaining the bond, Emerson worked to develop his own "private" park. Perhaps to demonstrate to the governing powers in Hutchinson how valuable public parks could be, Emerson kept ownership of the parkland but opened it to the public, and thousands of locals visited the park every year. The establishment of a park system was certainly a sticking point for Emerson in 1912, as he also suggested that a state park would be desirable on a forty-acre tract on the southwest side of the Hutchinson Reformatory grounds.[144]

Along with philanthropy, Emerson worked on several senatorial issues in 1912. He was instrumental in the creation of a unified board of regents for state colleges, and he worked to repeal the state inheritance tax laws. He was successful in these efforts. However, since his first day as a senator, Emerson had envisioned bringing the state fair of Kansas to Hutchinson officially. In 1912, he was at last successful in securing the passage of a bill establishing Hutchinson as the official site for the Kansas State Fair. In 1913, the bill finally passed and was signed by Governor Hodges. The bill stated that Hutchinson would give the fairground lands to the state in return for the state providing financial support for the fair and allowing Hutchinson exclusive rights to use the name the "Kansas State Fair." In a letter Emerson wrote to Kansas secretary of state Charles Sessions, Emerson voiced his pride in getting the state fair to Hutchinson, acknowledging that Topeka had fought bitterly to retain the Kansas Free Fair but at the same time needling the "Topeka boys" about their "county fair" now that the state fair was in Hutchinson.[145]

Emerson worked relentlessly as a senator to have Hutchinson named the official home of the Kansas State Fair. *Reno County Museum Collection.*

Gentle ladies and gentlemen crowded the midway of the Kansas State Fair in Hutchinson and marveled at the oddities, goods and attractions. *Reno County Museum Collection.*

Perhaps Emerson was celebrating his senatorial victories, or perhaps he just liked to speed, but whatever the reason, one day in October 1912, Emerson and friends were out in the countryside joyriding. At the same time, a Mr. Milligan and family were parked beside the rode enjoying lunch. Milligan's small son and dog were playing in the road. Suddenly, Milligan heard a car roaring down the road. He said it was speeding and weaving side to side. He grabbed his son, but the dog remained. Unfortunately, the car ran over the dog. Enraged, Milligan jumped into his one-hundred-horsepower special car and ran down Emerson, who was driving a Pierce-Arrow. Upon being confronted with running over poor Milligan's dog, in his defense, Emerson explained he never saw the dog. Speeding seemed to be a passion of Emerson's.[146]

The state fair of 1913, now officially in Hutchinson, must have been a marvel, showcasing agricultural equipment, produce, livestock and, of course, entertainment and food of all types. Visitors were treated to surrey races and an indoor boat ride. However, amid all the frivolity, Kansas and the Midwest in general were experiencing one of the worst droughts in recorded times.[147] Therefore, it's no wonder Emerson became interested in the feasibility of irrigation in Reno County. Indeed, raised a farmer, he began to build his own irrigation systems on his land.[148] This early interest in irrigation would prove incredibly valuable in Emerson's other land acquisitions in the future.

Governor Hodges appointed Emerson to be regent for the Kansas State Teachers College in Emporia for an interim position from March 18, 1913, to June 30, 1913. Emerson, who had helped to set up the unified regents system in the previous year, now extended that same support to a new law setting up a unified State Board of Administration to govern state institutions of higher learning. This new board of administration replaced the regents system in 1913.[149] It was a remarkable achievement for Emerson to be involved with the governance of higher learning even with his limited formal education.

It was probably a good thing that Emerson only served for about three months as regent for the college in Emporia, as toward late 1913, he was once again called on to bail out another struggling enterprise, the Western Straw Products Company. He had been one of nine original directors and held 45 of the 3,500 shares of stock at that time. Board members of the company, together with the Commercial National Bank and the Hutchinson Commercial Club, contacted Emerson for his experience and business acumen. The company was struggling, and Emerson quickly took charge and reorganized the company as the Hutchinson Box Board and Paper Company. Emerson discovered that about $400,000 had already been invested in the company and determined that $40,000 needed to be raised in two weeks in order to keep it afloat. The *Hutchinson Gazette* of October 7, 1913, termed it "Hutchinson's habitual hustle" when Emerson and the board issued preferred stock in the company to successfully raise that much in only two weeks. Emerson once again assembled experts in the industry to advise him on how to increase production and turn the company around. It quickly became apparent that although there was an adequate supply of raw material, there were not enough good outlets for its wallboard products. The production of wallboard was successful, but not quite enough. It was at this point in 1914 that Emerson became aware of a defunct egg case filler plant in Omaha, Nebraska. He immediately made the connection that if the straw board company had the machinery from the egg case filler company, the company would have a built-in outlet for its raw materials. So a charter was made on September 21, 1914, for the Hutchinson Egg Case Filler Company to be incorporated with a starting capital of $34,000. The egg case company would be a subsidiary of the Hutchinson Box Board and Paper Company and rented land from the boxboard company on which to construct a manufacturing plant. By October 1914, egg case fillers made of straw byproducts were being manufactured and sold by the Hutchinson

These very early postcards show the Western Straw Products Company, which was built in 1909. *Reno County Museum Collection.*

company. Emerson had once again found a solution to pull a failing business out of the mud. However, it wasn't a totally smooth transition, as various groups struggled for control of this company for quite a few years to come.[150]

While fully immersed in all his businesses and other interests, Emerson remained devoted to his family. In 1914, he purchased a house at 925 North Main, built in 1887 by John Campbell for the Leidigh family, very early Hutchinson grocers.[151] It was a rather modest-looking house from the exterior, but the inside had grand rooms and extra-wide halls. The living room was so big for the time that some referred to it as a "ballroom." The living room had a majestic fireplace and big glass doors that led into a sitting parlor. A kitchen was at the very back of the home. The second floor had very wide halls and four bedrooms.[152] It was a grand house and may have whetted his appetite for the next home Emerson would build.

Being senator and president of so many companies, Emerson was still tied to his early agricultural roots. Often as a younger man, Emerson had tended herds of cattle, and so when in 1914 he became interested in establishing a purebred dairy cattle herd, it seemed relatively natural. He wanted to replenish herds owned by local dairy farmers with his purebreds.[153] However, in Topeka, far from his agricultural roots, Emerson must have seemed a ball of energy in the senate. Throughout his two terms, he served on many committees and as chairman of the committees for Penal Institutions and State Affairs. While serving as chairman of the Commerce Committee in 1915, he introduced no fewer than twenty separate bills. Some of those included an act to establish city courts; an act for the protection of fruit and shade trees; several acts providing for the Kansas State Industrial Reformatory in Hutchinson, such as the establishment of a greenhouse and a twine plant; and an act to provide a sanitary committee to examine and license retail butchers. Emerson was paid $64.80 in mileage for his 1915 year in the senate.[154]

Although politics played a big role in Emerson's life during his years in the senate, he was also passionate about history. This was evident by his involvement with the Kansas State Historical Society. He was elected a lifetime member by the board of directors on October 19, 1915. This was to be a lifelong passion and relationship, as he was reelected three times to serve on the board and served continuously through 1927.[155]

In 1915, Emerson began negotiations with the Arkansas Valley Interurban Railway (AVI). Prior to 1915, the AVI ran from Wichita to Valley Center, Sedgwick, Newton and Halstead. The AVI wanted to continue its lines into Hutchinson, but a fight ensued regarding on which lines it would enter the city. The Rock Island already had lines in Hutchinson as well as Emerson's Hutchinson Inter-Urban Railway (HIR). After negotiating with Emerson, the AVI decided to enter the city on Emerson's lines, running on tracks along Carey Boulevard that would be jointly owned by Ark Valley Interurban and Emerson's HIR. To accommodate this, Emerson extended the HIR tracks to run east down Avenue A and one mile east past Larabee Flour Mill on Lorraine Street. The Arkansas Valley Interurban would meet the tracks there and then enter into the city on the HIR tracks. From that point, the Inter-Urban went west on Avenue A to Main Street and then turned north on Main Street. Finally, it reached 2nd Avenue, where its Hutchinson terminal depot was located. Emerson prevailed once again, and on December 20, 1915, the first car of the Arkansas Valley Interurban entered Hutchinson on his tracks and the first passenger service began the next day.[156]

Rail transportation was not the only form of transport in which Emerson was involved. The world was taking to the air as aviation technology soared by leaps and bounds since the Wright brothers had flown the very first sustained flight with a powered, controlled aircraft in 1903. Pioneers in the industry across the world were experimenting and improving on this new, fantastical science, and the flutter of its wings had captured the imaginations of the once little town of Hutchinson. Emerson's sister Eva and her husband, W.E. Albright, farmed land that Emerson owned. The land was just off the southwest corner of Avenue G and Halstead Street. The aviation bug caught Eva around 1915 when pilot Clarence "Mickey" Morean came to Hutchinson with airplanes owned by the Barnes Auto Company. Eva's imagination was immediately sparked. She convinced Emerson to set aside some of his ground that they farmed southeast of Hutchinson for an aircraft landing field. A couple of hangars were erected on the land, and a gas pump was installed to refuel the planes when they made pit stops at this rural, makeshift early airport. The airfield, which became known as the "Albright Field" or "Albright Farm," was composed of one hundred acres of Emerson's farmground and was 2,100 feet long and 1,800 feet wide.[157] Emerson surely saw the writing in the clouds himself at this time—his sister Eva certainly did—and with her persuasion helped to put Hutchinson on the aviation map for the future.

The whirlwind year of 1915 ended. Emerson had introduced his final bills during his second term as a senator, indulged his passion for history and secured the immediate future of his Hutchinson & Northern Railway Line. The year 1916 promised a whole new set of challenges on the horizon for him.

Emerson must have felt the need to establish central offices for all his ventures around this time. So in 1916, he designed an office building to meet his specifications at 127 East Avenue B. Located at the corner of Avenue B and Poplar Street, this handsome, airy, two-story building served as the headquarters of the Carey Salt Company.[158] The building most certainly shared housing of the office needs for Emerson's many other businesses and his political functions as well. There is not a more perfect example of Emerson's frugality and "waste not, want not" mentality than the type of construction materials used in building his new office: he reused pieces of old wooden crates that at one time were used to hold Carey Lily Table Salt and "Carey-ized" product in the joist areas of the ceiling.

In the January 1916 edition of the *Industrial Refrigeration Journal*, Emerson stated that he was paid $3.00 a day while a senator and his hotel bill was $3.50 per day. With his second and final term in office ending in 1916, Emerson relates that he "could make no progress as a politician." He went on to say:

> *In fact, I am not a politician—I am a plain, ordinary businessman. If there is anything that I take pride in it is that I am a businessman and have a moderate success among businessmen and that I have their respect and their confidence. There is nothing in politics that appeals to me, or that I will tell my children about with pride, but it is business achievements that I am proud of.*[159]

Emerson ruled over his empire of businesses in his headquarters at 127 East Avenue B. *Conard-Harmon Collection.*

Emerson oversaw the staff of his many enterprises from his office at the rear of the main floor of his office building. *Conard-Harmon Collection.*

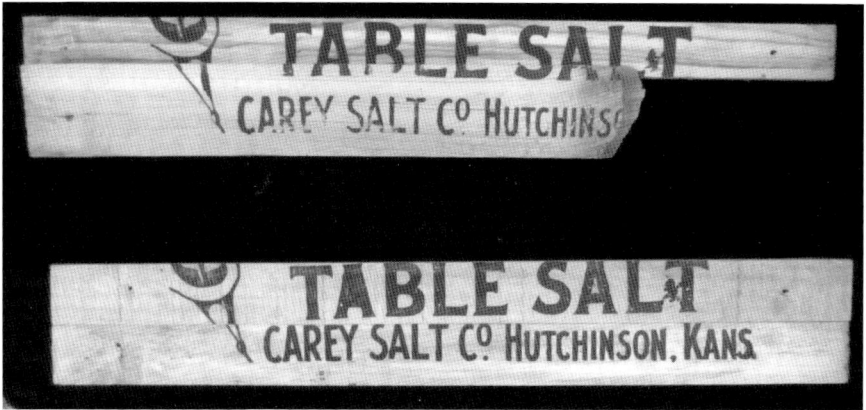

These wood pieces held up insulation in the ceiling of Emerson's Carey Salt Company headquarters. *Photograph: Reno County Museum Collection; original wood pieces courtesy of Brian E. Davis and Anne Lauer.*

And with this statement, Emerson rather humbly expressed his views of his eight years in the senate. As the official Kansas State Fair still comes out to play in Hutchinson, Kansas, 106 years later, Hutchinson residents would beg to differ with Emerson's views of his enormous achievements as the senator representing the Thirty-Sixth District.

It was probably a good thing when Emerson ended his eight-year political foray, as he stumbled into a new industry in 1916 when he became the proud owner of the local Hutchinson newspaper the *Hutchinson Gazette.* Warren Foster began publishing the weekly newspaper in 1890 supporting Populist issues.[160] From about 1908 to 1916, it became a daily newspaper. Harry A. Lill owned the paper from 1908 until he finally sold the struggling newspaper to a stock company in 1912. The paper continued with various editors and management inefficiency and ran as an independent paper politically but mostly supported the Democratic Party. Ownership eventually transferred to Emerson and co-owner Elijah Rayle while attempting to collect on a loan. Readership, however, had been flagging, and it fell to Emerson to work his magic on yet another struggling business.[161]

In October 1916, Emerson again showed both frugality and ingenuity when he came up with a plan to control grass growth in his two parks, Carey Park and Carey Lake. Emerson bought seven hundred head of sheep and divided them between the two properties. The *Hutchinson News* referred to the sheep as "mowing machines." Emerson planned to let the sheep graze

Right: Emerson Carey wound up his fruitful state senatorial career in 1916. *Reno County Museum Collection.*

Below: Emerson owned the *Hutchinson Gazette* from 1916 to 1924. This issue is from Sunday morning, November 10, 1918. *Reno County Museum Collection.*

over the winter to keep the weeds down and to save him money on mowing expenses. He then hoped to sell the sheep in the spring and reap a profit. Sheep were a natural solution to a costly problem and a logical choice due to Emerson's extensive experience with sheep from many past ventures raising herds.[162]

CHAPTER 7

BOXES, BAGS AND TROLLEYS

1917–1920

ife progressed in leaps and bounds in Hutchinson and for the Carey family throughout the years of 1915 and 1916. However, trouble had been brewing outside Carey's somewhat insulated town since 1914. When the Archduke Franz Ferdinand of Austria and his wife were assassinated while visiting Sarajevo, Bosnia and Herzegovina, the rest of the world erupted in war. The final spark that drew the United States and, thus, Hutchinson into what would become the Great War was the May 7, 1915 sinking of the British ocean liner *Lusitania*, which had carried 128 Americans on board. Although the United States attempted to remain neutral for two years afterward, on April 6, 1917, the United States finally jumped into the fray by declaring war on Germany. As Hutchinson's Company E and other companies trained and began to ship out, forty-six-year-old Emerson was to play a different role in the war. Kansas governor Arthur Capper advised President Woodrow Wilson to appoint Emerson as fuel administrator for Kansas. As fuel administrator during World War I, Emerson regulated the use of and set prices for coal and oil, with the goal of preserving these fuels for the war effort. With his vast and successful business experience, knowledge of the coal industry and overall toughness, Emerson was a wise choice for this appointment. While administrator, he ordered "lightless" Thursday and Sunday nights for Kansas in 1917. With this order, many businesses' lighted signs and unnecessary streetlights were darkened. Later, Emerson enforced shortened operating hours for businesses across Kansas, not always to the delight of some business owners who sometimes operated later in the day. He collaborated with the Coal Operators' Association to curtail strikes and lockouts and to encourage storage and even distribution of coal. During this time, a plan was launched to raise funds to maximize wheat production for the war effort; Emerson quickly became an enthusiastic supporter of this plan.[163]

Despite Emerson's best-laid plans as Kansas fuel administrator, he struggled to procure the coal necessary to meet Kansas's most modest needs. Emerson was aware of a coal shortage in the city of El Dorado in December 1917. In an attempt to curtail this shortage, Emerson asked the Santa Fe Railroad to let the city have one car of coal designated for Santa Fe in its yards. Santa Fe refused because it only had two cars. The people of El Dorado learned of the coal cars and raided one of the cars, getting the contents of one-third of the car before being run off by the railyard police. Emerson responded to this desperate need by convincing a paving company to give up a car; he also asked and received a car of coal from the Missouri Pacific Railroad. He then had two cars of coal diverted from Hutchinson delivery to El Dorado. He also found two cars destined for a Colorado iron company and was able to transfer those to the "fierce" situation in El Dorado. Through Emerson's skillful handling of the tense circumstances, he diffused the problem and filled the coal needs of El Dorado's desperate citizens.[164]

Many other towns also suffered when their supplies of fuel dwindled as shipments of coal were reduced and supplies were stored instead for the war effort. Newspaper headlines often read, "Kansas Towns Shiver." The prevailing attitude was that "Emerson Carey expects to become the Garfield of Kansas, the fuel dictator."[165]

In January 1918, headlines read, "Coal Situation in State Is Critical" and "Big Shortage in Cars," which only meant more trouble for Emerson as fuel administrator. Trying to diminish the problems, Emerson urged communities to report to their county chairman before the situation turned critical. The county chairman would then report the needs to the fuel administrator's office. Emerson stated, "We must appreciate that we are at war and that we may be called upon to suffer many inconveniences to which we are not accustomed."[166]

In March 1918, Emerson took steps to prevent the shortages of the previous winter. Emerson urged the people of Kansas and the counties to store coal during the summer. He suggested to all to place orders for coal whether they needed it or not. He urged the dealers to place large orders and, as soon as the orders came in, to deliver the coal to the consumers for storage. Emerson set the prices for the summer months and urged the mines to stay open all summer. Emerson said his goal was that by September 1, 50 percent of the winter need for coal would already be in the consumers' bins and yards.[167]

Somewhat hypocritically, while Emerson forced everyone else to tighten their belts in support of the war, on September 19, 1918, he himself was arrested for speeding, with a trial to be held later that day. Emerson's passion for speeding caught up with him once again.[168]

When Emerson accepted the appointment as fuel administrator, one can only imagine that his thoughts strayed back to that day long ago when he gazed on the larger-than-life tomb of Abraham Lincoln. His feelings of patriotism and righteousness came bubbling back to the surface; however, with the power he waged for the short time he was administrator, there were a few others who didn't see it that way and clearly felt that Emerson had taken advantage of the wartime system. Another fuel administrator accused Emerson of hogging all the rail cars himself to supply coal for his salt industry and collaborating with his brother-in-law W.D. Puterbaugh, who was "head of the largest coal producing mine in Arkansas and Oklahoma," to supply him with an excess of coal. This other administrator claimed that grain and corn were rotting in Texas and cattle were starving because there were no rail cars available for transporting the grain and corn, all while Emerson had access to an abundance of rail cars.[169] Whether the accusation was fair or not, Emerson remained the fuel administrator until the end of the war. On December 20, 1918, United States fuel administrator Harry Garfield in Washington, D.C., sent Emerson a letter and one dollar as a token of the country's appreciation for his services during the war.[170]

Although his responsibilities as fuel administrator would have commanded much of his time, with Emerson no longer a senator, he surely would have felt flush with free time to release his ample energies. He turned his attentions once again to his growing industrial empire and other outside interests. In 1917, he installed a quadruple effect vacuum system of the Ray type in his salt plant, which now had a production capacity of two thousand barrels per day. His Carey Salt Company was the only plant in the world at that time to have this type of salt manufacturing system. Emerson's ice plant produced eighty-five tons of ice per day, while his cold storage plant could hold one half million cubic feet of produce or other cold stock.[171]

Additionally, in 1917, Emerson organized the Carey Real Estate and Investment Company as a holding company for all the real estate that he controlled. By now, Emerson had amassed substantial landholdings. Some

Coal was still being used to fire the boilers at Carey Salt Company's East Plant, as evidenced by the coal cars. *Reno County Museum Collection.*

land was acquired for investment, some for farming and some for sites for his various businesses, and the remainder he used for miscellaneous purposes.[172]

Although his landownership was vast and spread out, Emerson had sunk his roots deeply and securely in the city of Hutchinson. It was very evident in the fact that he and his family were staunch members of the Christian Church. Always entrenched in his business affairs, his business associates were certainly well-known and well-received visitors to the Carey home, as the Careys hosted an annual dinner for company executives.[173] Emerson continued to extend the Carey family into the agricultural aspects of Hutchinson when, in 1918, he purchased an additional herd of 1,500 sheep.[174]

Growth and expansion continued in the business end of Emerson's life in 1918. It was a good year for the Hutchinson Box Board and Paper Company, as it now had two hundred employees. Sometime that year, Earl E. Widner bought a parcel of land from Emerson that was "prairie, raw and rough, and infested with buffalo wallows," with plans to turn it into a perpetual-care cemetery.[175] Indeed, the first recorded interment was in 1918. Effie Webb was the first interment at the cemetery, having passed on February 14, 1918, at the age of twenty-four, possibly having succumbed to the Spanish flu that was ravishing Kansas that year.[176] This land contract was made with the intent for Widner to pay Emerson with a portion of the proceeds of the sale of each plot. Widner was president of the Modern Burial Park Company of Springfield, Missouri, which owned and managed College Hill Memorial Lawns in Wichita and Green Lawn in Springfield, Missouri. With his experience, Widner was able to sell quite a few lots, but apparently Emerson never received payments to his satisfaction or per their contractual agreements. Not long after the establishment of this new Fairlawn Cemetery in Hutchinson, Widner moved to Springfield to manage the Green Lawn Cemetery. H.H. Brinsmade took over the management of Hutchinson cemetery. The land returned to Emerson, and like it or not, he was now the proud owner of the Fairlawn Cemetery.[177]

It had to have seemed portentous that the transfer of ownership of the cemetery went from Widner to Emerson in 1918 as tragedy was about to strike. The year 1919 began with much sadness for Emerson and his family when his beloved wife, Anna May Puterbaugh, passed away on January 3 at the young age of fifty-two. Anna had been suffering from rheumatism since 1893 and had never quite recovered. Emerson said of Anna, "I contribute a great measure of any success I have made to her splendid judgement, universal cooperation and inspiration."[178] The three older Carey boys were "boys" no longer but men now, as Howard was twenty-eight, Charles was twenty-six and William D.P. was eighteen. Only Emerson Jr. remained a boy at age thirteen.

Emerson had a bit more bad news in 1919. The Winchester Packing Company obtained its own twenty-ton refrigeration machine and so no longer needed the resources of the Carey Ice Plant. Although perhaps not a large loss, it still meant a loss of income and control for Emerson. His cold storage business had been piping ammonia gas to the Winchester plant for its refrigeration needs.[179] Soon another small yet somewhat humorous blow hit Emerson. Late one evening as Emerson drove home from the office, he turned the corner at Avenue A and Poplar. He felt a jolt and heard a screeching sound as the gray Marmon automobile he was driving came to a halt. It was a very prestigious auto because the brand had managed to win the very first Indianapolis 500 open wheel auto race. Emerson's Marmon was more than likely a Model 34, built from 1916 until 1925. Marmons had a reputation for their smooth ride, but that was not the case for Emerson.[180] As Emerson looked out, he saw a tire lying in the street. He knew the tire was his as the front left corner of the car was far too low. Emerson's car ended upright, square on the street railway track, and the streetcar had to wait. Soon a service car showed up, the mechanic had the tire back on the Marmon and Emerson was off to the races again.[181]

As if these occurrences weren't bad enough, a more serious event took place toward the middle of 1919. Workers across the country were uniting to demand wage increases and better working conditions. One group at that time was the Industrial Workers of the World (IWW). Known for being more radical than other similar worker support organizations, the IWW incited worker strikes and boycotts and distributed propaganda. Emerson's rise as an up-and-coming industrialist somehow came on their radar. In June 1919, a conspiracy was discovered targeting thirty-two leading citizens of Hutchinson, including Emerson and George Gano, a wealthy local grain man and the president of the Hutchinson Chamber of Commerce that year. The IWW attempted to blackmail these men to attain their goals with a plot that consisted of dynamite and sabotage. It was suspected at the time that Hutchinson was possibly a district headquarters for the radical IWW revolutionaries. Nothing came to fruition with this threat, and authorities sought to capture the culprits.[182] These unfortunate incidents coupled with the loss of his beloved Anna May must have made Emerson feel that luck was against him in 1919.

Although the loss of such a strong figure in their mother and wife must have been quite a blow, Emerson and the family pushed on with their usual strength. Emerson plunged himself back into work that same year when he and James Lee Dick, a longtime Carey Salt Company manager, founded the Hutchinson Bag Company. Its main purpose was to make bags for Emerson's salt company but also to make bags for the nearby flour industry. On a lot at the corner of Avenue C and Poplar Street, construction began in November of that year, and completion was planned for the first part of 1920. Dick was to be president, and the company would employ thirty to forty women sewing cloth bags. The lot covered a half acre, and the semi-fireproof, one-story building was to be 165 feet by 132 feet. The walls were to be 72 percent made of windows for lighting, and between building construction and equipment, the cost was set to be $30,000. According to Dick, the total investment would be about $300,000 to $400,000[183] (about $4,063,000 to $5,417,000 with inflation calculated to today's market).[184] Essentially created to keep the costs of salt bags in-house, this huge investment from Emerson for a relatively small offshoot business really indicated the vast amount of wealth he had acquired by this time. (The company, which became known as Hubco, wasn't officially incorporated until 1923.)

Now a new president of the Hutchinson Bag Company, back in the chilly world of ice and cold storage, in 1919 Emerson was also president of the Kansas Ice Men's Association.[185] Control of the Hutchinson Box Board and Paper Company, however, was an entirely different story. As noted previously, various groups had been wrestling for control of the boxboard company since its reorganization and charter in 1913. Emerson's business acumen once again came through as he had been receiving stock of the company for services he rendered, and he ended up with voting control of the stock. When other stockholders became disgruntled with the direction the company was taking, Emerson bought their stock from them. Some of the dissatisfied stockholder groups sued. They accused Emerson of abusing his position as director of the Hutchinson Box Board and Paper Company by contracting with the Hutchinson Egg Case Filler Company and allowing the egg case company to profit at the expense of the boxboard company. The suit alleged that the contract between the companies stipulated that the boxboard company provide the product to the filler company at a cost of $21 per ton while the going rate at the time was $50 to $70 per ton. The suit also alleged that if the boxboard company was not able to fulfill the orders, the company had to purchase boxboard from other markets at the going market rate. Both of those stipulations would certainly, as the suit alleged, have caused losses at the Hutchinson Box Board and Paper Company while allowing the Hutchinson Egg Case Filler Company to prosper. Additionally, they charged that Emerson was able to acquire boxboard stocks from the unhappy stockholders at substantially lower prices. Emerson's attorney, Judge Charles M. Williams, countered that when the contract between the two companies was made, the Carey family owned only $6,100 of the $350,000 worth of stock of the boxboard company and only $6,000 of the $32,000 worth of stock of the egg case filler company. The remainder of the stock was owned by other stockholders. He went on to argue, therefore, that with Emerson's smaller investment in the two companies, Emerson's only intents were to create a market for the boxboard company and still allow both companies to survive. Williams said that it was only when the egg case filler company wasn't succeeding at first that the stockholders became disgruntled and Emerson bought them out. Because of that, Emerson and his sons ended up owning all but $5,000 of the company. In the end, no fraud was found.[186]

Breathing a sigh of relief upon being exonerated of any wrongdoing in the boxboard company management, Emerson went full force with the company, organizing the boxboard and the egg case filler company into the new Emerson Carey Fibre Products Company on December 30, 1920. Two major products the company manufactured were Atlas Board and Bison Board, popular brands of fibre wallboard. By 1919, the Fibre Products Company had completed construction of the manufacturing plant building and had installed new manufacturing equipment. Back in 1906, the boxboard company had an output of wallboard of 500,000 feet, valued at $15,000. In contrast, fast-forward to 1919, and the Fibre Products Company was now manufacturing 550,000,000 feet of wallboard with a value of $22,000,000. Emerson estimated that one-third of all the wallboard production in the United States was being shipped to dealers west of the Mississippi, incurring higher freight costs, as his competitors were located farther east and thus had farther to go. Shrewdly, he calculated that with the creation of the Emerson Carey Fibre Products Company manufacturing wallboard farther west, there would be lower freight costs, making the product cheaper for customers in the West. A.D. Steward was the vice president and general manager, while Frank McCook was the sales manager.[187]

It seems an abrupt change from a fibre company to a cemetery, but it really exemplifies the wide variety of financial holdings that Emerson controlled simultaneously. However, by 1920, two hundred burials had already taken place at the Fairlawn Cemetery. About six hundred lots had been purchased with memorial markers. Emerson himself erected a $4,000 monument for the Carey family plot. The lot prices ranged from $500 to $2,000 in the 1920s.[188] Emerson once again showed his philanthropic nature when he gave lots in the cemetery to his employees.[189]

Another of Emerson's concerns, the Hutchinson Inter-Urban Railway, was in somewhat of a quandary at this time. After Emerson took control of the railway in 1914, the railway began an upward swing and began to show some positive profits. However, by the time 1919 rolled around, the flagging company was backsliding and started to show some losses. Emerson told a concerned committee that the company was "on the rocks" and that "we're going worse in the hole every year." He stated that workers who were making twenty-seven cents per hour were now demanding more. He also divulged details about company finance, admitting that the company was $120,000 in debt and had lost over $12,000 in the two years prior.[190]

Indeed, the beleaguered transportation system was being chipped away on quite a few fronts, just as Emerson described. These included rising

The Emerson Carey Fibre Products Company is in the center, and the Carey Salt Mine is in the upper right corner, circa 1930. *Reno County Museum Collection.*

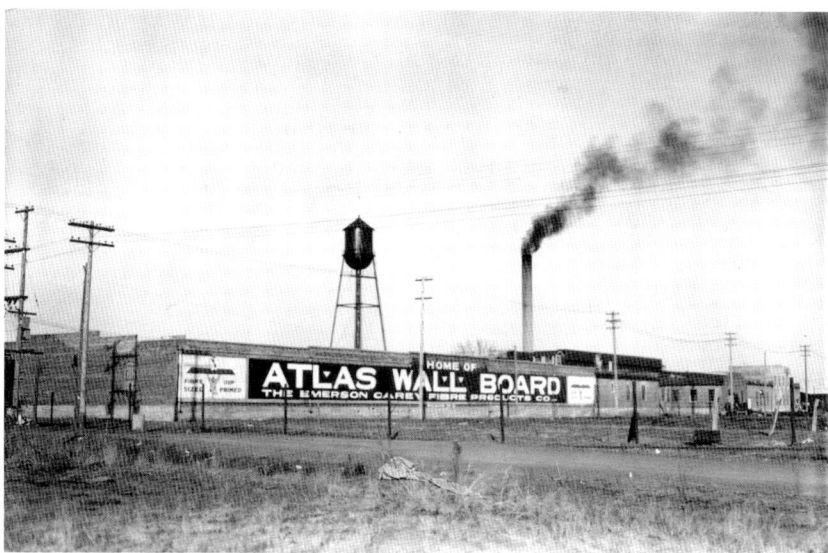

The Atlas Wall Board brand was one of the main products produced by the Emerson Carey Fibre Products Company. *Reno County Museum Collection.*

91

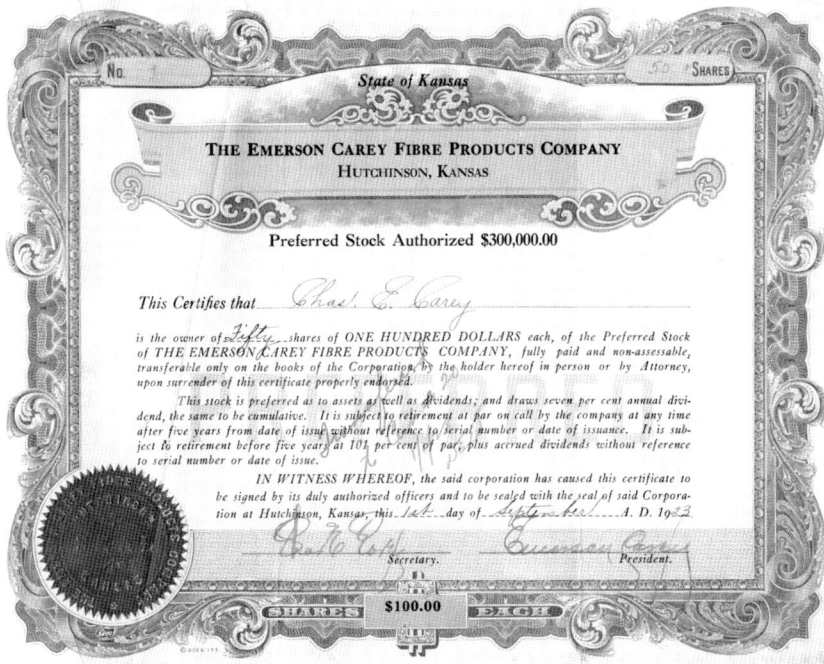

Charles E. Carey owned fifty shares of the Emerson Carey Fibre Products Company, as indicated by this 1923 stock certificate signed by his father. *Reno County Museum Collection.*

operating costs, demands of the now unionized workers, explosion of affordable automobiles flooding the market and competition from jitneys.[191] A sizable market arose of unregulated automobile operators who usually charged a jitney—a slang term for a nickel—for a ride; thus, the vehicles became known as "jitneys." Often the jitneys stalked the streetcar routes, stealing fares by providing a more individualized and private service. The jitneys also carried small groups and eventually began to charge ten cents. How wrong Henry L. Dougherty of New York, a well-known financier and operator of public utility properties, was when, as quoted in the *Public Service Magazine* of 1922, he said, "There is of course a gradually growing appreciation of the jitney situation, but there is much to do to impress this on the public. It is idle to believe that a rubber-tired vehicle that uses gasoline as fuel and an independent power plant in each vehicle can successfully compete with the electric railway." An unknown author in the same publication in which Dougherty expressed his viewpoint made the following observation: "Especially it is being understood that the streetcar and the jitney bus cannot

These six Hutchinson Inter-Urban streetcars list their destinations at the top, including "Ave. A. & Reformatory," "Fairgrounds" and "S. Main & Depots." *Reno County Museum Collection.*

co-exist."[192] Emerson wanted the city to prohibit the operation of ten-cent jitneys and force the jitneys to charge twenty-five cents at the minimum. He demanded that the city "stop this unfair competition by jitneys."[193]

Emerson also wanted to raise fares on the streetcar line from five to seven cents. The committee agreed with him on both accounts, and he filed an application with the Public Utilities Commission to raise fares in June 1919. However, it wasn't long before Emerson saw the writing on the wall and sought offers from the Kansas Public Utilities Commission to take over this railway.[194] The downward trend of the Hutchinson Inter-Urban Railway continued after 1919.

Something in 1919 that began with a more positive note than the downward-spiraling Hutchinson Inter-Urban was the creation of a new real estate development known as Careyville, although it, too, was fraught with difficulties after its formation. Emerson platted out and promoted this housing development on the east side edge of the city.[195] It's likely that Emerson named the development Careyville as a nod to the name locals

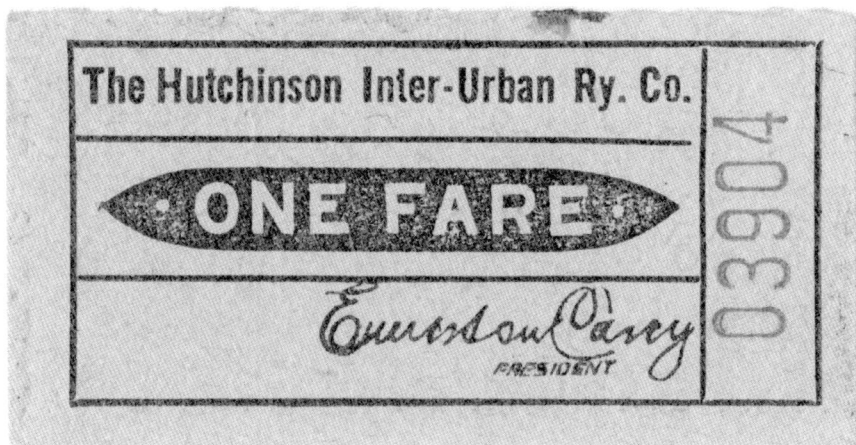

After paying from five to ten cents, passengers received a ticket like this for a ride on the Hutchinson Inter-Urban Railway from 1906 through 1932. *Reno County Museum Collection.*

had given to his complex of industries and buildings located in the Avenue C and Main area (where his coal, hides, ice, cold storage and salt plants were all operating). He even named three of the streets in Careyville after his children: Howard, Charles and William. With Emerson's benevolent attitude toward his employees and his philanthropic efforts around the city of Hutchinson, it seems a logical assumption that Emerson developed the area for his employees, seeing it as a way to offer benefits to them and provide for their welfare. As a further example of this, in 1920, Emerson donated two lots in Careyville for the formation of the Careyville Mission of the First Avenue Baptist Church, which was the only church in Careyville. An ice cream social at the mission, presided over by Dr. Horace Cole, took place on July 16, 1920, with about twenty people in attendance.[196] Perhaps Emerson may not have consciously intended to turn Careyville into a "company" town, but certainly something similar developed due to the fact that many Carey industry employees did live in Careyville. However, within one year, the Hutchinson City Commission passed an ordinance of annexation for Careyville. Emerson fought this by seeking to have Careyville incorporated as a third-class city instead.[197] The fight went all the way to the Kansas Supreme Court. In 1921, the court ruled that Careyville was part of Hutchinson, and steps were then taken to annex the Careyville area into the city.[198] Perhaps as a conciliatory concession to Emerson, in 1922, the city gave him the contract for lighting the streets of Careyville.[199]

Looking east, the Arkansas Valley Interurban Railway tracks ran alongside Carey Boulevard on the north side of Careyville. *Reno County Museum Collection.*

In 1920, Emerson installed a power generation system at the East Plant. Again, Emerson used steam already being generated in order to produce salt. The East Plant generating station was able to produce enough electrical power that it could power not only the salt plant but also the AVI in Hutchinson and the recently platted Careyville subdivision. The city commission wanted Carey Salt to take out a franchise to produce power, but Emerson did not want to do that and said if he had to take out a franchise then he would be compelled to go after the entire city. He was producing and selling power at three cents a kilowatt hour, as compared to five cents charged to Hutchinson by the United Water, Gas, and Electric Company. At that time, the AVI was buying power from three separate companies to supply its route between Hutchinson and Wichita: Carey at three cents, United at five cents and Wichita at ten cents per kilowatt hour. There was a vague threat implied by the *Hutchinson News* that if Carey Salt applied for a franchise, the United Water, Gas, and Electric Company might sue Carey Salt for infringement.[200]

The rear of the United Water, Gas, Electric Company faced Cow Creek in January 1923. *Reno County Museum Collection.*

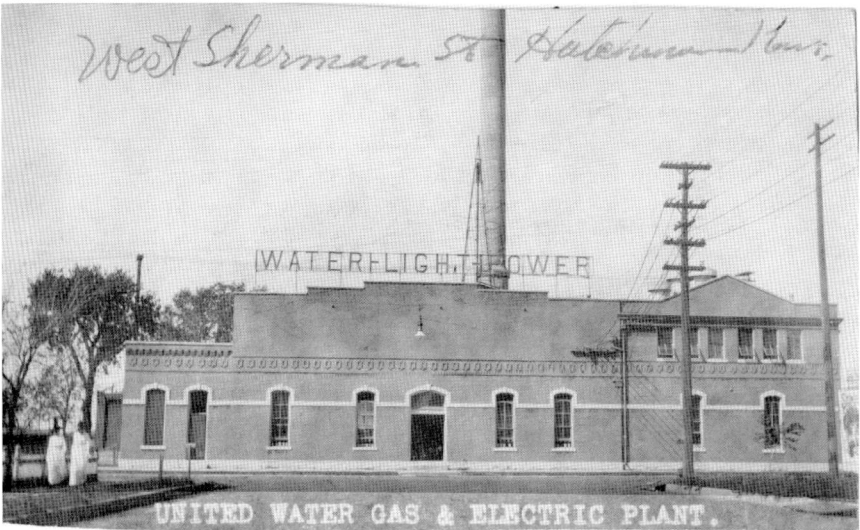

The United Water, Gas, Electric Plant battled with Emerson's People's Water, Light, and Power Company over rights to operate in Hutchinson. *Reno County Museum Collection.*

With the platting of Careyville, Emerson cemented his meteoric rise to industrial tycoon. The Hutchinson Gazette Printing Company published a special marketing newspaper insert promoting southwestern Kansas around 1920. The *So-we-kan* (South-Western Kansas) summed up Emerson's vast empire quite nicely with the following list of businesses:

The Carey Salt Company
The Gazette Printing Company
The Hutchinson Box Board & Paper Company
The Hutchinson Inter-Urban Railway Company
The Carey Real Estate & Investment Company
The Carey Ice and Cold Storage Company
The Hutchinson Egg Case Filler Company
The Hutchinson Bag Company[201]

Emerson Carey signed this 1924 stock certificate for the Salt City Building, Loan, and Savings Association showing the company had $5 million authorized capital. *Reno County Museum Collection.*

The *So-we-kan* claimed that the *Gazette*'s circulation had now risen to 9,500; however, the newspaper was still operating at a loss and would continue to do so for several years, despite Emerson's magic touch and best efforts.[202]

The *So-we-kan* had compiled the list of Emerson's business holdings a bit too soon, however, as on March 8, 1920, Emerson incorporated the Salt City Building, Loan, and Savings Association. He and his son Howard J. were the two largest shareholders, and Emerson's youngest brother, Claude Carey, was the secretary and treasurer that year. In 1920, the company had corporate assets of $51,000, but eight years later, in 1928, assets would rise to $547,000 (in 2018, with inflation calculated in, that equates to about $658,652 and $7,064,364, respectively).[203]

The Roaring Twenties now consumed the nation, and Hutchinson was no exception. This decade continued to be expansive and mostly successful for Emerson. He had been out of the senate now for four years and must have missed the political wrangling because he turned to politics once again in 1920. Emerson wanted to be part of the Kansas delegation to the Republican National Convention that year. But it was not be, and Emerson failed to secure a spot within the delegation.[204]

CHAPTER 8

THE AFFLUENT LIFE

1921—1922

S ince 1908, Emerson had been an integral part of the local
Hutchinson Country Club, being a member of the first board of
directors and its very first president.[205] As the club was located
adjacent to the Solvay Process Company, the Solvay Company began to
encroach more and more on the club's location. It is also widely believed
that the emissions and waste from the chemical plant were having a negative
effect on the grass and trees of the golf course.[206] Emerson and the board
knew that the time had come for the club to move to significantly larger and
more exclusive quarters. In his usual fashion of acting and solving problems,
Emerson was able to convince the Solvay Company to purchase the country
club land. The next step was a bit more difficult to solve—where to relocate.
The board needed to find a new site for the growing club. Emerson knew
of eighty acres of land west of Hutchinson, north of 43rd Street, owned by
Elmer Dukelow. Emerson referred to it as the "Schaeffer property." Emerson
felt the north eighty acres would be perfect for the new country club and golf
course. In fact, Emerson thought the land he was interested in was "one of
the most beautiful layouts for a golf course he had ever seen." The other
members of the board of directors felt differently. They were looking at
land, also west of the city and only about two and a half miles away from the
Schaeffer property, owned by Levi Rayl. Emerson felt that Rayl's land wasn't
the best suited for a golf course as there were too many water features. This
was another one of the rare cases in which Emerson did not get his way; the
board voted against him and chose the Rayl property for the new country

Above: The Hutchinson Country Club at Eleventh and Halstead in 1918, about three years before it moved to new quarters. *Conard-Harmon Collection.*

Left: Looking smart in his golfing attire, golf remained a passion for Emerson throughout his life. *Mike Carey Collection.*

club and golf course. Not one to bellyache over a lost fight or to lose out on what he knew to be a good deal, Emerson purchased the eighty acres he had recommended for himself.[207]

Right away, Emerson set about developing his new, beautiful property, bordered by cottonwood trees that had been planted in 1881, as his very own private nine-hole golf course. At this time, only the Carey family and family friends had the privilege of playing on this private course, which Emerson named "Willowbrook." Emerson planted several thousand more trees, including willow, elm and ash. Armed with his previous knowledge of and experience with irrigation, Emerson installed aboveground irrigation pipes to bring water to the course and keep the greens and trees lush and healthy. The pipes not only brought much-needed water but, painted green, also served as an enclosure for the property. The landscape was designed by renowned landscape designers Hare & Hare of Kansas City, and the golf course was laid out by designer Perry Maxwell of Oklahoma City. There were rustic bridges crossing Cow Creek, the stream that meandered through the property; benches for weary golfers; and imposing, lighted gates at the entrance. The golf course became the first and only privately owned course in Kansas at the time. On the back of the Willowbrook golf course scorecard it read, "No playing for money permitted. It is grand enough to play golf without gambling."[208]

Playing golf at Willowbrook with Emerson must have been very similar to when he played with friends and family at the Carey Lake golf course. Keith Rishel, operator of the Fairlawn Cemetery in later years, discussed golf at Carey Lake:

> *Dues were about $55 a year....It had real good lemonade, I used to play with Emerson and [Emerson Jr.] June, for a lemonade. Emerson frowned on any kind of gambling at all, however to play for a lemonade was legitimate. We were always careful around him, too, that we didn't say any words that weren't just exactly right. Nobody even considered drinking or anything like that in those days.*[209]

Emerson was so enamored with the Willowbrook property that he built a new home there for himself and his family. His white pine Colonial-style home, "The White House," cost $15,000 to build in 1921 ($194,000 in today's markets) and had its own pumping and light plants. There were servants' quarters in the back of the house. The basement had a large dressing room with a fireplace, showers and a billiard room. The first floor had a sun parlor,

Emerson's home in Willowbrook was the crowning symbol of his success as an industrial magnate. *Hutchinson/Reno Chamber of Commerce Collection.*

living room, dining room, kitchen, sleeping porch and shower. The second floor had guest bedrooms and a shower.[210]

With the beauty of Willowbrook at the top of Emerson's mind, it's no wonder that in 1921, he donated two hundred acres of land at the south end of Main Street to the City of Hutchinson to be established as a park. This land was southeast of the existing Riverside Park. His only stipulation was that the city be able to raise $5,000 each year for maintenance and upkeep of the park. The city agreed, with plans to put levies in place to raise money for the agreed-upon maintenance expense.[211]

Emerson's philanthropic efforts with the city were admirable and untarnished. However, another charitable action descended rather quickly into a bit of controversy for Emerson and his Carey Real Estate and Investment Company. In 1920, the company offered to furnish the school board of Careyville a rent-free building for use as a school. A building went up quickly at the corner of Center and Charles Streets in Careyville and was named Lakeview. One year later, the board received an electric bill from

SCENE IN CAREY PARK, HUTCHINSON, KANSAS—25

Emerson's donation of two hundred acres of land in 1921 led to the creation of Hutchinson's Carey Park, as seen in this later photograph. *Reno County Museum Collection.*

the Carey light plant along with a notice saying that the company would now be charging rent for the school. The board became very dismayed and threatened to close the school, saying the students would have to go to Grandview or Sherman schools. There were only eighteen students at the time. When Claude Carey, the Carey Real Estate and Investment Company's secretary, was questioned about the situation, he replied that the company had offered to furnish the rent-free building only as a temporary, emergency measure while other solutions were found for a school building for the students.[212]

Several events of note occurred in Emerson's life and in his beloved city in the year 1922. In May 1922, the City of Hutchinson held a formal opening ceremony for Carey Park, the land that Emerson had donated. Residents came out to enjoy the newly christened park with picnic baskets and the municipal band played, to the delight of everyone who attended. Major W.L. Brown was elected as the very first park commissioner, and trees and shrubs were planted to supplement the mature cottonwoods growing along the river.[213]

Emerson's newspaper, the *Gazette*, was still hanging in there, and by 1922, the printing company offshoot of the paper, the Mutual Press, was operating a bit more successfully than the paper itself.[214]

By 1922, Emerson's cold storage facility required some expansion and additional space was added to accommodate fifty railway cars. His ice plant, which originally was made of wood frame construction, also needed a more durable permanent construction and a new, separate location. Emerson constructed a $100,000 two-story brick building at the ice plant, which allowed the daily capacity of ice to be brought up to one hundred tons.[215]

CHAPTER 9

SOARING TO NEW HIGHS
AND DIGGING TO NEW LOWS

1923–1931

The year 1923 was a pivotal one for Emerson. He further expanded his Willowbrook holding in 1923 with eighty acres south of 43rd Street. The dam in Cow Creek was put there by Carey's brother Arthur to generate electricity and to divert water from Cow Creek. The water ended up almost surrounding the south eighty, eventually giving that area the name Island Park, and then became known as South Willowbrook. Emerson obtained these eighty acres from the Wilson family in a trade; Emerson ran electricity to the Wilsons' home near the property, which they had never had before, and had the county road that ran from Highway K96 to the property named "Wilson Road." James Lee Dick, who had been vice president at one time of the Hutchinson Inter-Urban Railway and was Emerson's partner in the Hutchinson Bag Company, was the first to build a home in Island Park. The second home was built by Dr. Starrett.[216] Emerson's son Howard recalled, "Emerson and [Emerson Jr.] June visited Great Britain when William was at Oxford as a Rhodes Scholar. They visited him in England and they played golf in Scotland. Island Park wasn't built until after this, and they tried to copy some of the ideas that they got in England on the Island Park course."[217]

Even though Emerson's business interests had ranged far—coal, cement, lime, stone, hides, ice—he never forgot or strayed too far from his early agricultural roots. In 1923, he was the chairman of the agricultural committee of the Hutchinson Chamber of Commerce. As chairman, Emerson hoped to stimulate young children's interest in breeding purebred

Emerson promoted the breeding of purebred cattle and can be seen standing in the doorway of the cattle barn on the Kansas State Fairground. *Reno County Museum Collection.*

livestock, particularly cattle. He and his youngest son, Emerson Jr., offered two $250 prizes to the boy or girl owning the greatest number of purebred cattle raised from a single cow at the end of five years. He was involved in loaning over $14,000 to a calf club during this year as chairman.[218]

Besides expanding Willowbrook and officially incorporating his Hutchinson Bag Company in this year, Emerson opened one of his most lasting legacies, the Hutchinson Rock Salt Mine. Emerson and his son Howard had been prospecting for a rock salt mine site as early as 1912, but it wasn't until April 8, 1922, that his plans to sink a shaft to mine salt were announced.[219] Emerson was almost sixty years old in 1922, and his oldest son, Howard, was thirty-one, so Emerson, showing much confidence in his firstborn son, gave Howard carte blanche on developing the Hutchinson mine. Howard picked the Allen & Garcia Company, a new engineering firm from Chicago led by Andrews Allen and John A. Garcia. A site was chosen about one and a half miles east of the evaporation plant, and the shaft would cost about $300,000 to build. Emerson offered 7 percent of preferred stock to help finance the construction of the shaft, and the venture was oversubscribed in just two days. By June 1922, work on the shaft began, and it continued until August, when a vein of water was tapped. Deep-sea diver George Nelson was hired to seal off the vein so that construction could be continued, and at last on December 15, 1922, a salt vein was tapped at 400 feet. The actual shaft was completed by March 1923 at a depth of 683 feet, and an 85-foot hoist tower was erected. On June 23, 1923, Kansas governor Jonathan Davis had the honor of pulling the switch that hoisted the first load of salt.[220]

Interestingly, President Harding was in Hutchinson on June 23, the same day the mine was dedicated, to give a speech on agriculture. Emerson could have picked any day to open the mine, but he picked the day Harding was in town. There has always been speculation that Emerson invited Harding to join the mine opening. However, it is rumored that Harding did not want to upstage Davis in his own state. Indeed, Harding was not on the list of prominent figures who attended the mine opening. Harding did, however,

The Carey Rock Salt Mine opening on June 23, 1923. *Conard-Harmon Collection.*

stop on Rayl's Hill just outside Hutchinson and cut a ceremonial swath of wheat. There is a granite roadside marker to commemorate the day.[221]

Almost immediately, a price war over rock salt developed between the American Salt Company at Lyons and the Carey Salt Company. Prices went from $1.50 per ton to about $0.50 per ton. Eventually, a compromise was reached, and the company's position was assured. (American Salt went into receivership in 1928, perhaps due to this price war.)[222] Emerson had just steered the Carey Salt Company in an entirely new direction that would not only expand his business but also further solidify his reputation as a salt magnate.

Key to Emerson's entire salt operations, and all commodities industries in general, had always been shipping and transportation. Emerson intimately understood just how important the railroads were to his business. It was one thing to extract salt but quite another to get that product to consumers. So, it was logical that Emerson had his eye on a certain Hutchinson & Northern Railway (H&N). Back in 1912, a man in the insurance business, W.S. Thompson, chartered the Hutchinson & Northern Railway company. In the ensuing years, Thompson had allowed the company to become idle, and Emerson, ever on the hunt to capitalize on a good deal, saw the benefits of taking over the inoperative railway. He planned for the H&N to serve as a switching line, running from his salt evaporation plant to the rock salt mine; he also foresaw that the railway would tie into the Hutchinson & Southern Railway that ran through Kingman, Kansas, to Ponca City, Oklahoma, and north through Salina to Fairbury, Nebraska. Success again occurred for Emerson when, on August 1, 1923, the Kansas Public Utilities Commission authorized the H&N to be operated as a terminal railway, allowing him to charge fees for switching services.[223] Emerson's control of the H&N sparked a suit by the American Salt Company. Already a staunch rival due to Emerson's plunge into the rock salt mining world, American accused Emerson and the Carey Salt Company of the very thing that Emerson had fought Joy Morton for in court back in 1903, alleging that the H&N was not a true railway and was established only to obtain "refunds" from all the major railways coming into Hutchinson.[224] This suit that went before the United States Interstate Commerce Commission battled for years before a final decision was reached.

Incredibly, Emerson's spirits were not hampered by the H&N debacle. He continued to advocate for industrial growth for the Hutchinson community by urging the creation of an industrial zone free of property taxes. During 1923, Emerson was disappointed that the city council did not allow the

The small building (*left*) is the original hoist house, and the large building is the mill building of the Carey Salt mine. *Reno County Museum Collection.*

Solvay Process Company to remove itself from the city limits, which he hoped would have sparked a possible reopening of the Solvay plant. (The Solvay Process Company closed its doors in 1921, just three years after the end of World War I, stating that production costs were too high.) His forward-thinking idea was to draw businesses to Hutchinson by giving tax incentives and lowering the taxes that existed at the time for industry.[225]

As the rock salt mine must have surely moved to the forefront of Emerson's business interests during 1924, he divested himself of one of his least successful business ventures, the *Hutchinson Gazette*. The paper was purchased by W.Y. Morgan, editor of the *Hutchinson News*. The *News* turned the *Gazette* into the *Herald*, a morning newspaper. Despite his golden touch with his other holdings, Emerson never was able to make a go of the paper and took a significant loss when he at last sold the *Gazette*.[226]

Howard Carey, now thirty-three years old, and his brother William D.P., now twenty-three, built their own homes in Willowbrook, joining their dad. Now, with his sons close by in his beloved Willowbrook, with its pristine golfing greens, Emerson continued to finetune his golfing skills. Already quite adept at the game, Emerson proved it even further, somewhat spectacularly, when, in February 1924, he beat the famous baseball player George Herman "Babe" Ruth Jr. by one stroke at the Hot Springs Country Club in Arkansas. The Babe finished out with a score of 89, while Emerson's final score was 88.[227]

At its peak during World War I, the Solvay Process Company employed about eight hundred men and had its own route on the Hutchinson Inter-Urban Railway. *Reno County Museum Collection.*

Emerson also began platting the Sunset Heights addition in 1924. Bordered by 23rd Avenue on the north, 20th on the south, Monroe Street to the west and Adams Street on the east, the addition contained two mid-block parks and a street aptly named "Carey Place."[228]

In May 1924, Emerson applied for a passport. He and his son Emerson "June" Jr. traveled on the *Olympic* ocean liner to Europe to visit William D.P., who was studying at Oxford, and also to do some sightseeing. They had plans to visit England, Scotland, Ireland, Belgium, Germany, France, Italy and Switzerland. Emerson returned to the States with June, bringing with him a new love for all things English, Scottish and Italian.[229]

Although Emerson traveled a good deal in 1924, he still was thinking about the community. That year, Emerson donated his old home at 925 North Main to the women of Hutchinson for use as a clubhouse for the Hutchinson Civic Center.[230] Emerson himself proposed that the club's name be the Hutchinson Civic Center. His deed of gift for the house stated the requirements that "membership be composed of white women, and no club which is secret, partisan, or religious shall have the club privileges extended to them, as to those whose aims are civic, musical, literary, fine arts, or philanthropic." Mrs. Edward E. Yaggy was the temporary chairman, and formal organizational proceedings were to begin once there were 300

Emerson donated his old home at 925 North Main to be used as the Women's Civic Center in 1924. *Reno County Museum Collection.*

women signed up to join. By November 15, 143 women had signed up, and notices in the paper encouraged women to join.[231] The organization would become known as the Women's Civic Center in the future.

Emerson's donation of his Main Street home for the Civic Center was a wonderful, generous gesture based on a building. However, while the Main Street house was getting a new lease on life, another structure in Hutchinson was coming to the end of its life in 1925. On February 27, Reno County government staff noticed cracks appearing in the courthouse. Over the next few days and weeks, the cracks expanded dangerously, to the concern of county officials. By March 2, the cracks had become bad enough that court proceedings were halted and all participants sent home. On March 3, the Carey Cold Storage building immediately to the south was evacuated as a precautionary measure due to concerns that the grounds were settling and fears that the courthouse might collapse onto the Carey buildings. Built in 1901, the courthouse was already nearly twenty-five years old and too cramped for the growing county offices. As a safety precaution, the county departments were scattered throughout the city to various office spaces, including the Great American Life Insurance Company, the Commercial

National Bank, the YWCA offices and the Arkansas Valley Interurban Depot. During the early stages of the cracking, the city contemplated buying the courthouse, as there was a need for a more permanent city hall building. However, the condition of the building had deteriorated too far. Emerson made it known at that time that he was willing to buy the courthouse and the grounds around it for the appraised value.[232] This situation would continue to involve Emerson in the coming years.

Six years had passed since Emerson's first wife, Anna May, had died. All four of his sons were grown; his youngest, Emerson Jr., was now a young man of nineteen. Perhaps feeling a bit of the empty nest himself, or perhaps while negotiating and interacting with the women of the Civic Center, Emerson once more entertained the thought of marriage. He married his second wife, Frances W. Sentney, on October 14, 1925.[233] It was fairly certain that Emerson knew Frances for a long time, as she was the widow of K.E. Sentney, who along with his brother C.N. Sentney, founded the Sentney Wholesale Grocery Company in 1909. K.E. and his brother had been frequent investors alongside Emerson in many ventures, including the packing business, the electric streetcar company and the soda ash plant.

Emerson was busy yet again in 1925 with an amazing variety of activities. He formally incorporated the cemetery he had received back from Earl

The impressive Reno County Courthouse at Avenue B and Main Street began to show cracks in 1925 and was razed in 1929. *Reno County Museum Collection.*

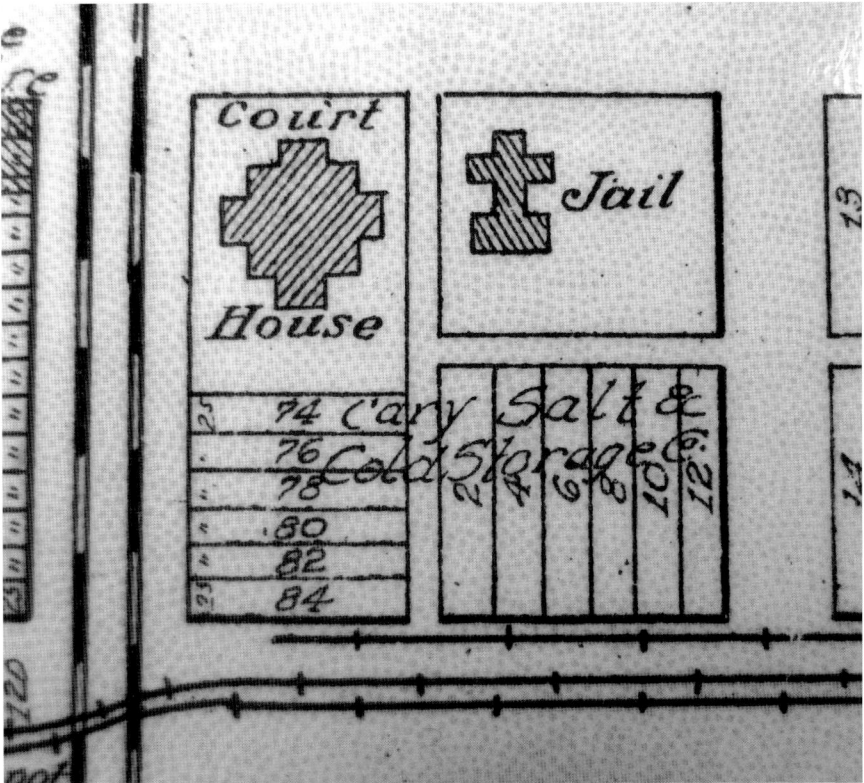

A section of the 1902 plat map showing the proximity of the Carey Salt and Cold Storage Company properties to the Reno County Courthouse. *Reno County Museum Collection.*

Widner into the Fairlawn Burial Park Association. Emerson officially terminated all salt production at his Avenue C and Main location. He continued to produce ice at this location, however, and by 1925, all of his ice production facilities ran completely by electricity.[234] The Kiwanis Club named Emerson "First Citizen of Hutchinson" due to all his charitable and distinguished service to the community.[235]

Emerson participated in a group that recommended routes for the United States highway system. Earlier in 1921, the Federal Aid Highway Act was passed, which encouraged road construction with matching funds across the country. The act focused on connecting state highways to create a more national system. As usual, Emerson had his fingers on the pulse of the action as he became involved in the state highway planning. In 1925, he was part of a delegation to Washington to divert some of the matching funds to Kansas.

Emerson and his second wife, Frances Sentney, relax at the "White House," 65 Willowbrook, in 1925. *Conard-Harmon Collection.*

He used his love of golf to help sway the opinion of Secretary of Agriculture William M. Jardin, also a golf lover. His persuasion, as part of the group, helped to establish the old Santa Fe Trail as U.S. Highway 50.[236]

After his success with the highway plans, Emerson's success continued when, on June 19, 1926, the Interstate Commerce Commission sided with him and his Hutchinson & Northern Railway, allowing the railway to operate as a switching line. The ICC granted "orders of convenience and necessity" to the H&N and ruled that no illegal action had been taken. This legal victory gave vast logistical access to Emerson's H&N, as it linked his mine, his evaporation plant and the entire eastern industrial district of Hutchinson with the Chicago, Rock Island and Pacific Railroad; the Atchison, Topeka & Santa Fe Railroad; and the Missouri Pacific Railway.[237] Where Joy Morton had lost his railroad battle against Emerson in court, Emerson proved triumphant.

Emerson must have felt quite vindicated by his win in the H&N case, and perhaps as a way to celebrate this victory, he built another nine-hole golf course in Island Park, the south eighty acres by Willowbrook.[238]

A year had passed since the Reno County Courthouse had been abandoned, and in 1926, the county sued Emerson for $200,000 for "gross negligence and reckless disregard for the rights of the county." The suit alleged that the courthouse was sinking and settling due to the Carey Salt Company salt brine wells that had been dug under and near the location of the courthouse building. This civil court case went on for a total of three years, with the state fire marshal eventually officially declaring the building unsafe for occupancy in 1928. The marshal described a circular depression in the soil with a three-hundred-foot radius that was situated east of the building, causing the courthouse to settle and sink in the center, in essence, breaking the building in two. But it wouldn't be until 1929 that the case was finally settled.[239]

While the crumbling courthouse gave Emerson a sinking feeling, his ownership of the Albright Airfield had to have given him a soaring feeling. Since about 1915, when the field first came into use, it had become a regular stop on many pilots' routes and was the site of many exciting aviation exhibitions by 1927. Through the 1920s, many famous pilots and aviation pioneers landed on Emerson's Albright Field, including Art Goebel, Martin Jensen, Roy and Clyde Cessna and Lloyd Stearman. Emerson's sister Eva was the airport's main operator now, and pilots enjoyed visiting with her on

In this photo taken prior to 1917, the Carey Ice and Cold Storage Company lies just below (south of) the domed courthouse. *Reno County Museum Collection.*

A Ford Tri-Motor owned by Standard Oil of Indiana sits on Albright Field in 1928. *Reno County Museum Collection.*

their short stops in Hutchinson. Air travel by this time was in its golden age, with barnstormers performing enticing, daring stunts. Advertisements often ran in the *Hutchinson News* in 1927, luring local daredevils with "Sky Rides! $1.00, Fri.-Sat.-Sund. only. Albright Flying Field. East of Reformatory. Big New Ships. Licensed Pilots. Using Skelly Products for Reliability."[240] The field was no longer a primitive, thrown-together air strip but was very close to becoming an established, official stop on aviation flight plans.

In 1928, Emerson was the chairman of the airport committee of the Hutchinson chapter of the National Aeronautic Association. The Transcontinental Air Transportation Company, under the direction of Colonel Charles Lindbergh, was searching for airfields throughout the country on which to establish passenger and airmail service. Emerson hoped to update and improve Albright Field to accommodate this new industry if it was acceptable to the representatives of the Transcontinental Company. Prior to 1928, Emerson received very little in the way of income from the use of his farmground as an airfield; there was no landing fee, and it cost only $1 to park a plane in the hangar. There was a guard, accessible fuel, oil, a telephone and a telegraph, but no radio was available in 1928. Emerson offered to lease the field to the city for $125 per month for a year. His sales department head at the Carey Salt Company, R.G. Streeter, was the chairman of the joint airport committee that was composed of the Hutchinson Chamber of Commerce and the National Aeronautic Association's Hutchinson chapter. Streeter urged the city to submit an $8,000 bond in the upcoming November 1928 vote to cover the cost of a lease, purchasing lighting equipment and other assorted maintenance costs. Emerson agreed to lease the land to the city if the bond was put up to vote and would not ask for back payment on the lease should the bond fail. Emerson told the city that should the bond fail, he planned to plant wheat on the land.[241]

In May 1927, tornados ravaged the Midwest, including Hutchinson. The Carey Salt East Plant sustained major damage and loss of life. Henry Strouse, a night boiler fireman, died when part of the boiler house collapsed on him. Carey Salt was able to make temporary repairs and get production back on track. Things were not as quickly recovered at the Solvay chemical plant. A 165-foot water tower was toppled when its five-thousand-gallon water tank came crashing to the ground.[242]

For all of Emerson's successes and well-played business deals, he was very wrong in one opinion that he held strongly in 1928. He wrote a letter that was published in the *Hutchinson News* on Saturday, June 23, 1928. In the letter, Emerson voiced his strong objections to building dikes on Cow

The large building (*left*) housed the Solvay Process Company offices. *Reno County Museum Collection.*

Creek. His entire letter was printed, in which he gave many reasons for his position. In his letter, he stated that Cow Creek "never does any material damage when it rises. It never has overflowed very many times where it caused any inconvenience....I cannot see that it matters to Hutchinson either way whether this stream is diked or not." Emerson went on to suggest that each individual farmer or property owner could ask for and pay a nominal fee to have his own individual dike built on his land, if he so desired. He stated that he didn't want that to occur at his Willowbrook home and that he didn't want to have to pay contractors and engineers and "have them all over his Willowbrook property." How wrong Emerson was when one year later in 1929, a monster flood occurred in Hutchinson. "The stream" (as Emerson referred to it), Cow Creek, overflowed its banks and crashed through downtown, all across the city and onto the surrounding farmland. Railroads were stopped when their tracks were washed away or the land beneath eroded away. Basements flooded by the hundreds, and even the *Hutchinson News'* printing press was inundated with water, causing the newspaper company to outsource its printing. The first bridge to cross the creek at the entrance to Willowbrook was also washed out by the raging waters of this devastating flood. The water reached from one to four feet in many areas, and damages were estimated to be over $1 million (about $15 million with today's inflation).[243] This was one rare case in which Emerson really had it wrong and had to eat his words.

Emerson and his sons became interested in the salt market in Louisiana. At this time, Emerson and Howard organized the Louisiana Development Company to allow the Carey Salt Company a chance to compete in the southern salt markets. Salt was to come from the Winn Parish salt dome, discovered in 1927.[244] Louisiana governor Huey P. Long and the State of Louisiana encouraged the expansion of the Carey Salt Company into Winnfield, Louisiana, in accordance with the state's industrialization program that was in force at the time. Long allowed a paved highway to be rerouted, giving trucks easier access to the newly proposed mine, and offered certain tax benefits to the company. Again, Emerson tapped Howard, who was now vice president of the Carey Salt Company, to oversee the development of the Winnfield mine. Once more, Howard picked the Allen & Garcia Engineering firm of Chicago to help design and build the mine. Because Howard used the same engineering firm as in the Hutchinson mine, many of the Louisiana mine's design features were similar to those in Hutchinson; for example, track gauge and mining equipment were the same. The plant and mine were built at a cost of about $500,000. The first test drilling began near the city of Winnfield in 1929, and the prospect of the new mine and new jobs must have been very exciting for the residents of Winn Parish.[245] However, a larger, more ominous event was soon about to take hold of Louisiana and the entire world.

The stock market crash of 1929 plunged the United States into the devastating Great Depression; however, Emerson and the city of Hutchinson seemed to shrug it off and pull through. The Reno County government's courthouse case against Emerson's salt company was finally dismissed when, on March 12, 1929, Emerson bought lots 58, 60, 62, 64, 66, 68, 70 and 72 on South Main Street and lots 1, 3, 5, 7, 9 and 11 on East Avenue B for $60,000, all of which included the courthouse and grounds. He was the highest bidder in the sale of this property. Emerson and the county ended up splitting the cost of the suit. Emerson eventually had the courthouse razed in 1929. In his typical style and showing his usual sense of midwestern frugality, Emerson repurposed quite a bit of the salvageable building materials from the courthouse. Parts of the slate roof of the old courthouse dome and some of the bricks from the courthouse were used in building a caretaker's cottage in Emerson's Fairlawn Cemetery. Two of the granite pillars that stood at the entrance to the courthouse were used in the construction of the cemetery's War Memorial.[246]

As further evidence of Emerson's and Hutchinson's seemingly impervious nature, in 1929, $35,500 worth of improvements were made in Emerson's Carey Park. With inflation calculated to the equivalent to today, that would be about $515,000—quite a sum to be spent on recreational pursuits when all over the country people were experiencing the worst economic depression of their lifetimes. A city swimming pool and a lagoon with rowboats for rental were added, and not too long afterward, a golf course and baseball diamond with bleachers were constructed.[247]

The city had plans for even more expansion and modernization. City officials made the decision to look at potential sites besides Emerson's Albright Airfield to provide land suitable for a new municipal airport. While the Albright farm was still in the running, there were five other sites being considered. The five included the Ghormley-Smith property, land at the Fernie Ranch, Rayl Hill land, the King Tract and land on the Carey Farm. Each had its pros and cons, but the two the city was most interested in were the King Tract and the Carey Farm. The King land was three miles from town center, reached easily by concrete roads, with proximity to the Rock Island and Santa Fe Railroads; Emerson's other land, the Carey Farm, was also about three miles east of the post office and had easy accessibility on

The Carey Park boathouse is at left center, and the bathhouse is in the background. *Reno County Museum Collection.*

Local residents enjoyed climbing iconic Rock Hill in Carey Park. *Reno County Museum Collection.*

an improved concrete highway, Route 50. On March 23, 1929, the city announced the decision to buy Emerson's 180 acres for $27,000. There was a bit of a disagreement over the valuation, as Emerson asserted that the land was worth $31,500. It may have been Emerson's influence and position in the community that swayed the city officials to purchase his tract. Also key was the fact that in the end, he offered free continued use of the existing Albright Airfield until the municipal airport was complete. Wasting no time and true to his word, as soon as the new Hutchinson Municipal Airport was completed and open for business, Emerson plowed up Albright Airfield in November 1930 and planted wheat.[248]

Many may have hoped that the opening of the new municipal airport might have brought jobs along with it. This may have been the case, but hardships were still being felt in the salt city. With so many men out of work during the Depression of the 1930s, Emerson's benevolent nature showed through once more as he tried to spread work in his various industries between as many men as possible.[249] Hard times affected everyone, however, and perhaps as a cost-saving measure, Emerson had gas installed at the homes in Willowbrook. Willowbrook had always had electricity, but in the past, the homes there were heated by oil, which was a far more expensive way of heating.[250]

Emerson survived the 1929 stock market crash and the tough year afterward. He and his son Howard, therefore, would have warmly welcomed the goods news of 1931, even though the effects of the Depression would be felt for many more years to come. Their Louisiana mine found salt on March 1, 1931. The Carey Salt Company leased the Winnfield mine from the Louisiana Development Company and shipped salt out under the Carey Salt name in that same year.[251]

Despite the Depression, or perhaps because of the Depression, the Salt City Building, Loan, and Savings Association was soaring. It carried assets totaling more than $830,000. During 1931, the president of the board was Howard J. Carey. Emerson stepped down to be a vice president, and Walter Boehm was also a vice president. C.C. Buchanan was the secretary, while George B. Dicus was the assistant secretary and J.D. Elder rounded out the officers as treasurer. The directors were C.M. Williams, J.H. Childs, Ralph W. Jones, H.S. Pegues and Will H. Shears.[252] Many of these men's names are recognized even today as some of the movers and shakers in Hutchinson. This is proof that Emerson, even at the age of sixty-eight, was well respected, admired and followed.

The news of the success of Emerson's Winnfield mine must have provided hope for Louisiana and Hutchinson. All eyes might have turned to him for

Opposite: Ads for the Salt City Building, Loan, and Savings Association, with Emerson as president, ran consistently in the *Hutchinson News* throughout the 1920s and early 1930s. *Reno County Museum Collection.*

Right: Emerson Carey, about 1930. *Conard-Harmon Collection.*

inspiration. In fact, Emerson gave an interview that year that was printed in the *Hutchinson Herald* on May 24, 1931. Emerson related the story of his past to the reporter: "He had to walk from near Canton, McPherson County because there was no train running there then, the Rock Island hadn't been built yet. 'I couldn't have come on the train if there had been one, because I didn't have the money.'" The writer estimated that in 1931, all of Emerson's various industries were valued at around $902,000. (In today's market, this would be almost $15 million with inflation.) The article listed Emerson's businesses at this time as "salt, ice, wallboard, egg case fillers, boxboard, Medisalt, cold storage plant, coal, building & loan association, printing plant, street railway, belt line railway, golf club, cemetery, a nursery, a realty concern, and the power plant."[253] Emerson had come quite a way from that boy who couldn't afford a train ticket—even if there had been one at the time. His life story would surely have inspired hope and pride in the *Herald*'s readers during a time of such financial hardships.

A big contributor to that $902,000 valuation of Emerson's wealth was the Emerson Carey Fibre Products Company, which by 1931 was wildly successful, thanks to Emerson's shrewd business maneuvers back in 1914.

The company was producing about one hundred tons per day of egg case filler, wallboard and various other fibre products. That year, the company merged with nine others to become the Central Fibre Products Company, with wallboard production facilities in Kansas, Indiana, Illinois, Missouri, Iowa and Nebraska. The company that at its beginnings rose from Hutchinson, Kansas's natural resources of wheat straw had long progressed from using only that and now used mostly wastepaper collected throughout the region.[254]

CHAPTER 10

THE FINAL YEARS

1931—1935

A significant sign that sixty-eight-year-old Emerson was in his twilight years was when he loosened the reins on the fibre plant, allowing son Charles full control. Charles moved into the role of president of the fibre company while Emerson stepped in the role of the chairman of the board of directors.[255] Emerson's health may have already been giving him cause for concern during the late 1920s and in 1930, as in 1931, he built a grand mausoleum in the Fairlawn Burial Park. The mausoleum was named Temple of Memories. This imposing granite structure with three wings and large iron doors was graced on the interior with marble floors and walls and iron grill work at the main vestibules. The main room boasted six large marble columns that flanked either side of the main entrance, which culminated in three elegant stained-glass windows at the end of the curved entrance. Even today, the elegance of the marble interior reflects the quiet, stately opulence of the taste of its builder. Emerson, ever the calm planner, had secured a final dignified resting place for himself and his family in his hometown of Hutchinson.

It is an unfortunate fact that Emerson knew that he had colon cancer for quite some time before his death. Surgery for colon cancer in this time was highly discouraged because of the extremely high death rate from infection. So instead, doctors started the patient on a treatment course designed to stimulate the body to defend itself from the disease. The treatment often included special foods and relief from stress with the goal of relaxation. This, in part, might explain Emerson's vast overseas travels in his later years.[256]

The ornate nature of the mausoleum at the Fairlawn Cemetery is still apparent in this 2018 photograph. *Marcotte Collection.*

The Fairlawn Cemetery mausoleum boasts an imposing entrance. *Marcotte Collection.*

Left to right: William D.P., Howard, Emerson, Emerson "June" Jr. and Charles Carey, about 1930. *Conard-Harmon Collection.*

On October 10, 1932, the Hutchinson Box Board and Paper Company, the Hutchinson Egg Case Filler Company and the Emerson Carey Fibre Products Company were all officially declared dissolved; they were replaced by the Central Fibre Products Company.[257] The old guard was being swept away by progress and growth. However, Emerson remained chairman through the end of his life.

The Carey Real Estate and Investment Company was pared down to only handling real estate and insurance in 1932, and in this same year, the Careys sold the company and it became the Wade Patton Insurance Company. The end of the line had at last come to the Inter-Urban Railway business, which had never fully recovered from its embattled state and also the Depression, when it ceased operations in 1932.[258]

The death of the industrialist, legislator, philanthropist and civic leader occurred in Hutchinson on August 17, 1933. It wasn't until after Emerson's death in 1933 that the Carey Salt Company was officially incorporated. The Carey Ice and Cold Storage Company was also officially incorporated in 1933 and the name was retained, with properties that included the ice plant at 226 South Main, Hutchinson; an ice plant in Sterling, Kansas; and branch sales that extended to fifteen nearby Kansas communities.[259]

Almost immediately upon Emerson's passing, a group of his friends and influential businessmen began to plan a memorial in his honor. A cenotaph

127

The interconnected letters H, I, and U serve as a logo on the side of this Hutchinson Inter-Urban streetcar. *Reno County Museum Collection.*

would be erected in Carey Park, the land Emerson had donated to the City of Hutchinson. In February 1934, some six months after Emerson's death, Ray Hockaday was named chairman of the memorial committee. Architect Otho McCrackin was chosen by the memorial committee to not only design the memorial but also redesign the park's meandering, haphazard drives. One of the key concerns was ample parking. McCrackin devised a plan where as many as three thousand cars could be parked in an emergency by using fields.

McCrackin submitted a tentative design of the memorial to the city for approval. In March, the finance committee, consisting of chairman V.M. Wiley, J.A. Davis, Brant Holme, John Starr and Ray Hockaday, was tasked with the challenge of raising the estimated $5,000 necessary to build the memorial. In their first meeting in Wiley's office, they planned a fundraising campaign to raise the necessary funds.

By August 1934, one year after Emerson's death, plans for the memorial were formally approved by the city commission. While the initial $5,000 had already been raised, the final plans called for additional funds, and a new chairman, Joe O'Sullivan, started a campaign to raise $1,000 more. At the same time, details for the memorial were released by O'Sullivan and McCrackin. The plans outlined a grand memorial with three tall arches of Indiana limestone. The same type of limestone had been used to create the World War I memorial in Kansas City, Missouri, which was still fresh on people's minds. A fountain was to be at one level along with a fifty-foot reflecting pool at a lower level with a waterfall between the two pools. The pools and fountains were to be lit at night. Descriptive lettering announcing the memorial was to be thirteen inches high. The entire cenotaph was to be set back one hundred feet off the existing Riverside Drive, would have a thirty-five-foot-wide drive circling it and was to be set just off the main gate to Carey Park on South Main Street.

In September 1934, $500 still needed to be raised in order to start construction. Foy Construction was awarded the contract to build the memorial, Stevens Plumbing was awarded the fountain project and Hartmann Foundry, known for its water pumps in Hutchinson, provided the pumps for the fountain. Shortly after construction began, unexpected changes of an unspecified nature were forced upon the financial committee. Another $400 needed to be raised, so the community was asked to donate. They could leave money at any financial institution. The Lions Club donated $50 to help fill the gap.

Other local businessmen wanted to donate goods and services instead of money. W.M. Hartmann of the Hartmann Foundry and Hartmann Pumps

The fountain in Emerson's memorial featured prominently in the center of the original entrance to Carey Park. *Reno County Museum Collection.*

donated the pumping equipment for the memorial fountain. Bill Wagoner of Wagoner Nurseries donated seventy evergreens of varying species. His donation was actually to the city parks department, but his intention was that they be planted around the entrance gate to Carey Park near the memorial.

On July 2, 1935, Hutchinson was given its first opportunity to see the fountains when it was announced by the memorial committee chairman that the fountain would be turned on and the colored lights displayed at 8:30 that night. The display consisted of colored lights that changed along with changing fountain patterns. Harry Stevens of Stevens Plumbing and parks commissioner R.B. McCarroll spent many hours working out the intricate patterns and colors to make the display not repeat for one and a half hours. They manipulated the fountain machinery located in an underground basement at the memorial until they perfected the display. That night, passengers in five hundred cars parked at the entrance to the park and witnessed the first lighting of the fountain.

By August 21, 1935, Governor Alf Landon had been asked to speak at the memorial's dedication. He tentatively accepted the invitation, saying it would be an honor to speak at Senator Carey's memorial dedication because "he was one of the fine, outstanding citizens of Kansas." An invitation to speak was also extended to Senator Arthur Capper. The formal dedication was scheduled for October 24.

Colored lights played along the fountain as part of the memorial cenotaph to Emerson in Carey Park. *Reno County Museum Collection.*

A dedication committee was formed and chaired by J.C. Dunlap. The first meeting took place on October 2 in the Wiley Tea Room, located in the iconic department store in Hutchinson's downtown. A parade was planned, to be accompanied by addresses by dignitaries and a multiple-band concert that was to be held that evening. As October 24 approached, people began to clarify their intentions to attend the dedication or abstain and for what reasons. A touching letter came in from Senator Clark Conkling of Lyons, who wrote, "Very sorry but I do not feel that I am able to attend. I am especially sorry because Mr. Carey was one of my most valued Hutchinson friends. He was never too busy to stop and talk of his early experiences in Rice County, where he herded cattle at the munificent salary of $10 per month and camp grub. He delighted in those days. But at 84 I find it necessary to conserve my strength and feel that I best stay home."

Around October 15, the Kansas Poultry and Egg Shippers Association announced its semi-annual meeting would be held in Hutchinson on October 24. Emerson had been a longtime member of the association, having sponsored the conference several times over the years. The president of the association wanted to give the members a chance to attend the memorial dedication.

The women at the Women's Civic Center at 925 North Main had a radio installed on October 23, 1935. They wanted to listen to the addresses and bands' performances held during the memorial service, and since some of the women were elderly, they thought this would be the best way to do so. The Women's Civic Center building had been donated to them by Emerson, and it's sure that in this way they could show their respect to him. Many businesses planned to be shut down from 3:00 p.m. until 6:00 p.m. in observance of the memorial dedication to allow their employees a chance to attend.

October 24, 1935, was a clear fall day, and after a parade down Main Street, people gathered at the memorial fountain, where a rostrum had been built for the speakers and honored guests. It was decorated in autumn foliage using leaves and sumac. Upon it were Kansas governor Alf Landon and United States senator Arthur Capper, as well as Hutchinson mayor D.J. Wilson and six senior Carey industries employees who had worked for Emerson the longest. Directly in front of the platform was reserved seating for the Carey family and close friends, and behind them was reserved seating for other dignitaries, such as railroad executives, industrial leaders and former state senators who served with Emerson. To one side was a special area reserved for all employees of Carey industries. A special platform was built for various church choirs from throughout the city, and across the reflecting pool was the joint Hutchinson High School and Municipal Bands. Around the outside of this was a circle of National Guardsmen. This was smartly done to help control the throng of people who came both to show their respect and to hear and see the dedication.

As the ceremony began, the band played and the choir sang an anthem of music, a tribute to Emerson. The colors were raised on a tall staff. An Episcopal minister gave the blessing, and then Judge Charles M. Williams, Emerson's old friend and business partner in many ventures, opened the ceremony with a brief account of the life of Emerson Carey. He then introduced Governor Alf Landon, who paid tribute to Emerson. Senator Capper was introduced, and he began his story of the life of Emerson Carey. He mentioned that the family came to Kansas in a covered wagon with only a nickel, that Emerson came to Hutchinson with only a quarter in his pocket and that Emerson had the courage to stick and hold on even in the toughest of times. Senator Capper concluded by saying, "If Kansas had more Emerson Careys, how our state would thrive and forge ahead."

After the distinguished speakers finished, the band began to play "The Star-Spangled Banner" and the National Guard's color guard lowered the flag. As the colors lowered slowly, the fountain of the memorial began to dance in a rainbow of colors, just as it was designed.[260]

Emerson Carey's legacy is still alive and well in Hutchinson, Kansas. Emerson's four sons—Howard J., Charles E., William D.P. and Emerson "June" Jr.—carried on his legacies by expanding his beloved Carey Salt Company. Sadly, after ninety-seven years, Emerson's beloved iconic Carey Salt brand is no longer being made under any name, although the company Compass Minerals owns the rights to the Carey logo and name. However, the mine still operates today under the name Hutchinson Salt Company. The Hutchinson Bag Factory (now Hubco), a company Emerson was directly responsible for creating, produces bags known worldwide to geologists as *the* sample bag to use. Incredibly, the straw board company, which Emerson saved, is still in operation in the same location. Today, the company is known as Sonoco Paper Recycling and produces recycled paper products. The exclusive Willowbrook operates as its own city and has even added a few more homes in the last few years, with thirty-five households, eighty-seven residents and a per capita income of $118,000. Hutchinson has proudly renovated Carey Park after struggling to maintain it for many years. The park now boasts the Salt City Splash water park, a zoo, a paved hiking trail, a golf course, baseball diamonds, several ponds and,

Emerson's four sons, *left to right*: Charles, William, Howard and Emerson Jr. *Reno County Museum Collection.*

of course, Emerson's memorial. A further extension of Emerson's legacy is the prestigious Prairie Dunes Country Club and Golf Course, designed by renowned landscape architect Perry Maxwell in 1935, the same designer who designed Willowbrook. It was through Emerson's passion for golf that he instilled in his sons the same love of golf that drove the creation of this links masterpiece.

How do you measure a man's true mark on the world in which he lived? The quick answer many might say would be wealth. Emerson's wealth was surely in the millions when he passed. However, wealth seems like such a shallow way of measuring a man's true mark on the world. Athletic achievement is another answer one might use to measure Emerson's legacy. He played baseball, but he really excelled at golf, winning many championships and promoting the sport whenever he could. With Emerson, though, golf seemed more of a hobby than an achievement. Business, then, would surely be Emerson's mark on the world. He was a very successful businessman who operated many companies and employed hundreds of people, which enabled many people to support their families. Is being a great businessman Emerson's true mark on the world? So many people are successful in the business world that in actuality, it seems quite common. So, perhaps Emerson's mark is his philanthropy. He donated land for parks, beaches for swimming and courses on which to play golf. He helped others in many ways; he raised money for the sick, gave ice to the poor and provided coal for the cold. Another of Emerson's lasting important legacies is the city of Hutchinson itself. His rapid expansion into many diversified industries at the turn of the twentieth century gave Hutchinson a huge advantage over most Kansas cities. His willingness to risk funds and in turn reinvest profits, instead of building his personal wealth, gave Hutchinson a powerful industrial surge that lasted one hundred years.

Any one of those achievements could be Emerson's true mark on the world. However, Emerson's true mark was inspired by a visit to President Abraham Lincoln's tomb way back in 1878. His mother impressed upon him Lincoln's honesty, integrity and righteousness. He then adopted those traits for the rest of his life and treated his fellow human beings fairly and equally. Emerson himself said it best: "You can't lay down a set of rules by which a man can make a lot of money. But the rules of honesty are few, simple and perfectly clear. Every man knows in his heart whether his deeds are worthy of his own commendation or not—and that is the only commendation that is worthwhile."

CAREYISMS

While researching the life of Emerson Carey, it became clear to both of us that Emerson was incredibly driven, shrewd and charismatic—a man of high integrity. However, what truly surprised and entertained us was what we came to term "Careyisms." These are quotes that Emerson made throughout his life, both in print and in his autobiography, that are at times sage, folksy, poignant and often humorous.

We have compiled a list of these Careyisms here, along with the approximate years in which he stated them and, if possible, the events in his life from which the expressions stem. We hope you enjoy them as much as we did!

Would Lincoln have done this? If the answer was "No," his conclusion was "Neither will I."
—Emerson's thoughts to himself upon seeing the tomb of President Abraham Lincoln in Illinois, 1878

I find experience is a dear teacher, but I am firm in the opinion that the old adage is correct that "fools will learn in no other way."
—after surviving the ordeal of living through the Oklahoma land rush, 1930

This was a fine experience but like the old woman that had several children and said she would not take $10,000 for any one of them but would not give 10¢ for another.
—also in regard to his experiences with the Oklahoma land rush, 1930

[I've seen] …many a fly make a bull waggle its tail.
—in reference to the threat to deter Emerson's attempt to enter the salt business, 1908

I have always found time to turn back to the soil.
—on buying a "sand hill" farm on which Emerson stocked cattle and pigs and hoped to raise a vineyard, 1886

I made no money but got a world of experience.
—Emerson discussing his conversion of the Underwood Packing Company building into an ice-manufacturing plant, 1896

The banks seemed to feel that I was a plunger.
—Emerson reminiscing in his autobiography about the diversification of his business affairs, 1930

I started my business in a very humble way and as I considered it, a very conservative way.
—Emerson reminiscing in his autobiography about the beginnings of his empire, 1930

You are wrong in your ruling, one of us have got to give in and it is not going to be me.
—on Emerson's fight to get the maximum freight bill passed in the senate, 1912

It is certainly remarkable to what extent some men will go to help their own personal end, no matter how much it might injure someone else.
—referring to Hale's attempt to slander Emerson's integrity and honesty, 1885

Never borrow money to buy something you don't need.
—talking about the financial bust of 1893

Nine times out of ten, a poor man cannot afford to pay interest.
—talking about borrowing money, 1890

Don't be bluffed out, if you are satisfied that you are right.
—a lesson Emerson learned when Frank Vincent threatened Emerson to keep him out of the salt business, 1902

The most profitable thing a man can do is just to stick.
—a lesson Emerson learned from experience with all his businesses, 1925

He must learn that you can catch more flies with molasses than you can with vinegar.
—quoted from a speech at a Kansas Ice Men's Association conference, 1905

I might be termed what you would call a "buttinsky."
—quoted from a speech at a Kansas Ice Men's Association conference, 1905

I think it is a great mistake not to know every detail of your business from the coal pile to the bank account.
—stated as a delegate to the First International Congress of Refrigerating Industries, 1908

I think one of the greatest mistakes the ice man makes is not to keep cool—always keep a piece of ice in your hat.
—as a delegate to the First International Congress of Refrigerating Industries, 1908

There is no doubt about the scripture admonition that "Brethren should dwell together in unity…" as applied to all manner of business as conducted today.
—given in a speech to the Western Ice Manufacturers' Association, 1905

I am a plain, ordinary businessman. If there is anything that I take pride in, it is that I am a businessman.
—given in a speech to the Kansas Ice Men's Association, 1916

It is grand enough to play golf without gambling.
—printed on the back of Emerson's Willowbrook golf cards, 1922

Everything I have I owe to Hutchinson.
>—Hutchinson News, *August 17, 1933, page 1,*
>*quoted on the death of Emerson Carey*

I paid 100 cents on the dollar.
>—*Emerson was extremely proud that he always repaid his loans in full.*
>*This was his stock phrase whenever he paid off a debt.*

NOTES

Chapter 1

1. Carey, "Autobiography of Emerson Carey," 1.
2. *Coffeyville Daily Journal*, November 11, 1909.
3. Michael Carey, interview with author, July 10, 2018.
4. Ploughe, *History of Reno County*, 33–36.
5. Carey, "Autobiography of Emerson Carey," 1.
6. Ibid., 1.
7. Carey interview, July 10, 2018.
8. Carey, "Autobiography of Emerson Carey," 1.
9. Digital Sterling. "History of Sterling." Sterling.digitalsckls.info/history-of-sterling.
10. Carey, "Autobiography of Emerson Carey," 1.
11. Stewart, "It Pays to Hang On," 2.
12. Carey, "Autobiography of Emerson Carey," 1.
13. Stewart, "It Pays to Hang On," 1.
14. Carey, "Autobiography of Emerson Carey," 1; Stewart, "It Pays to Hang On," 4.
15 Carey, "Autobiography of Emerson Carey," 2.
16. Stewart, "It Pays to Hang On," 3.
17. Carey, "Autobiography of Emerson Carey," 2.
18. Ibid., 3.
19. Author's recollection.

20. Carey, "Autobiography of Emerson Carey," 3.
21. Stewart, "It Pays to Hang On," 6.

Chapter 2

22. *So-we-kan*, 1920.
23. Carey, "Autobiography of Emerson Carey," 19.
24. *Hutchinson Herald*, November 29, 1884.
25. Carey, "Autobiography of Emerson Carey," 3; *So-we-kan*, 1920.
26. Carey, "Autobiography of Emerson Carey," 3.
27. Ibid., 7.
28. Ibid., 3.
29. Ibid., 5.
30. *Hutchinson News*, August 4, 1886.
31. Simpson, "Brief History of Emerson Carey's Carey Salt Company," 107.
32. Carey, "Autobiography of Emerson Carey," 4.
33. Ploughe, *History of Reno County*, 356.
34. Author's recollection.
35. Carey, "Autobiography of Emerson Carey," 4.
36. *Hutchinson Daily News*, November 5, 1887; Craig Miner, "A Place of Boom and Bust: Hard Times Come to Kansas," www.kshs.org/publicat/history/2011spring_miner.pdf.
37. Simpson, "Brief History of Emerson Carey's Carey Salt Company," 107; Fred Henny Scrapbook of Hutchinson newspaper articles, 49.
38. *Hutchinson News*, August 23, 1888.
39. Simpson, "Brief History of Emerson Carey's Carey Salt Company," 107.
40. *Daily News*, September 27, 1888.
41. Carey, "Autobiography of Emerson Carey," 5.
42. *Green's Hutchinson Directory*, 87, 88, 147.
43. Wikipedia, "Land Rush of 1889," en.wikipedia.org/wiki/Land_Rush_of_1889.
44. Carey, "Autobiography of Emerson Carey," 5, 6.
45. Ibid., 4.
46. Ibid., 7; Stewart, "It Pays to Hang On," 88, 89.
47. Carey, "Autobiography of Emerson Carey," 8.
48. *Kansas: The First Century*, 25.

49. Simpson, "Brief History of Emerson Carey's Carey Salt Company," 124.

50. Ibid.

51. Carey interview, July 10, 2018.

52. Carey, "Autobiography of Emerson Carey," 8, 9.

53. Carey Salt Scrapbooks, copy of charter, October 1893 and notes from 1894.

54. Carey, "Autobiography of Emerson Carey," 9.

55. This section relating to mortgage information is from a copy of an 1893 mortgage signed by Emerson and W.E. Hutchinson of the Valley State Bank, Carey Salt Scrapbooks, located at the Reno County Museum.

56. Carey interview, May 7, 2018; Carey Salt Scrapbooks, copy of charter of Carey-Puterbaugh Coal Company, September 28, 1894.

57. *Hutchinson City Directory*, 48; Carey Salt Scrapbooks, copy of receipt, April 1, 1896.

58. *Hutchinson Daily News*, December 26, 1893.

Chapter 3

59. Carey, "Autobiography of Emerson Carey," 9.

60. *Topeka Daily Capital*, November 15, 1908.

61. Author's recollection.

62. *Weekly Interior Herald*, June 7, 1902.

63. Wikipedia, "Refrigerator Car," en.wikipedia.org/wiki/Refrigerator_car, accessed June 14, 2018.

64. Reno County Museum artifact collection.

65. Connelley, *Standard History of Kansas*, 228.

66. Findagrave.com; Carey, interview, May 30, 2018. Nancy was originally buried at Eastside Cemetery but was later moved to Fairlawn Cemetery shortly after Samuel passed.

67. De La Praudiere, *Historical References of the City of Hutchinson*, 30.

68. *Hutchinson News*, May 8, 1887.

69. Ploughe, *History of Reno County*, 513, 514; *Hutchinson Gazette*, December 22, 1898.

70. Simpson, "Brief History of Emerson Carey's Carey Salt Company," 81.

71. *Hutchinson Gazette*, June 28, 1900.

72. Ploughe, *History of Reno County*, 344; *Hutchinson Gazette*, March 29, 1900.

73. Carey interview, May 30, 2018.

Chapter 4

74. Carey, "Autobiography of Emerson Carey,"

75. *Hutchinson Gazette*, April 18, 1901.

76. *Historical References of the City of Hutchinson*, 1931, 33.

77. Carey, "Autobiography of Emerson Carey," 9; Carey Salt Scrapbooks, 227.

78. Carey, "Autobiography of Emerson Carey," 9.

79. *Saturday Bee*, November 29, 1902.

80. *Weekly Interior Herald*, January 18, 1902.

81. This section is based on the following articles from *Hutchinson Daily News*, December 20, 1900; *Hutchinson News*, April 8, 1902; April 9, 1902.

82. *Hutchinson News*, April 1902.

83. Carey, "Autobiography of Emerson Carey," 10.

84. Simpson, "Brief History of Emerson Carey's Carey Salt Company," 27.

85. Ibid., 41.

86. Carey, "Autobiography of Emerson Carey," 12.

87. Ibid., 10.

88. Ibid., 13.

89. *Daily Independent*, July 10, 1902.

90. Baker, "Reno County Court Houses," 7–11.

91. Carey, "Autobiography of Emerson Carey," 10.

92. Ibid., 11; *Saturday Bee*, December 12, 1903.

93. Dal Liddle, *Hutchinson News*, September 27, 1987.

94. Ploughe, *History of Reno County*, 513–14.

95. Fred Henny Scrapbook of Hutchinson newspaper articles, 82.

96. *Ice and Refrigeration Illustrated*, 33.

97. *Industrial Refrigeration, Ice and Refrigeration Journal*, various issues between 1904 and 1919, babel.hathitrust.org.

98. *Kansas: The First Century*, 25; Hanes, "History of the Salt Industry in Grand Saline."

99. *Saturday Bee*, April 23, 1905.

100. Connelley, *Standard History of Kansas*, 2700; Ploughe, *History of Reno County*, 33–36.

101. Fred Henny Scrapbook of Hutchinson newspaper articles, 103.

102. Simpson, "Brief History of Emerson Carey's Carey Salt Company," 107–11.

103. Ibid.

104. Carey interview, May 7, 2018.

105. *Industrial Refrigeration, Ice and Refrigeration Journal*, various issues between 1904 and 1919.
106. *Hutchinson Bee*, March 4, 1905.
107. *Independent*, December 9, 1905.
108. *Cold Storage and Ice Trade Journal* (April 1905): 38; (May 1906): 35, 36; (March 1907): 23, babel.hathitrust.org.
109. *Wichita Beacon*, January 10, 1906.

Chapter 5

110. Carey interview, May 7, 2018.
111. Wikipedia, "Soda Carbonate," en.wikipedia.org/wiki/Sodium_carbonate.
112. This section about the soda ash company was derived from Carey, "Autobiography of Emerson Carey," 21–26; *Hutchinson News*, October 21, 1979.
113. Sheehan, *Salt City Industrial Review*, 3.
114. Simpson, "Brief History of Emerson Carey's Carey Salt Company," 101.
115. *Industrial Refrigeration, Ice and Refrigeration Journal* (April 1908): 139.
116. Fred Aldrich, "A New Face in the Kansas State Senate," *Topeka Daily Capital*, November 15, 1908, 3. www.newspapers.com.
117. Macdonald, *Prairie Dunes*, 9.
118. Carey, "Emerson Carey, and His Industrial Empire," 14.
119. Simpson, "Brief History of Emerson Carey's Carey Salt Company," 115–16.
120. Boyd, "History of the City of Willowbrook," ch. III.
121. *Hutchinson Daily News*, July 6, 1908.
122. *Hutchinson News*, November 21, 1908; Wikipedia, "White Motor Company," en.wikipedia.org/wiki/White_Motor_Company#White_steamer; *Hutchinson News*, September 23, 1908.
123. Welsh, *Hutchinson*, 127.
124. Carey, "Autobiography of Emerson Carey," 10; author's recollection. The Lillie quadruple effect vacuum pan was designed by S. Morris Lillie, hence the name. Emerson and others commonly referred to the system as the "Lily" system, with this spelling. This ultimately led to the naming and brand logo of Emerson's Lily Brand Table Salt.
125. Author's recollection.

126. Carey, "Autobiography of Emerson Carey," 12.

127. Simpson, "Brief History of Emerson Carey's Carey Salt Company," 83.

128. *Hutchinson Gazette*, April 3, 1909.

129. This paragraph about the 1909 packing plant is based on "United States Packing Company," *New York Produce Review and American Creamery* 29, 415; *Coffeyville Daily Journal*, November 11, 1909.

130. *Hutchinson Times*, January 15, 1909.

131. Simpson, "Brief History of Emerson Carey's Carey Salt Company," 116–24.

132. *Lawrence Daily Journal*, February 24, 1909.

133. Carey, "Autobiography of Emerson Carey," 13.

134. Sheehan, *Salt City Industrial Review*, 22.

135. Ploughe, *History of Reno County*, 513–14.

Chapter 6

136. Simpson, "Brief History of Emerson Carey's Carey Salt Company," 103.

137. Ibid., 116–24.

138. Ibid., 111.

139. *Hutchinson Gazette*, January 12, 1912.

140. Simpson, "Brief History of Emerson Carey's Carey Salt Company," 96.

141. Ulrich, *Carey Salt Mine*, 9.

142. Simpson, "Brief History of Emerson Carey's Carey Salt Company," 100.

143. *Hutchinson News*, June 27, 1912.

144. Simpson, "Brief History of Emerson Carey's Carey Salt Company," 111.

145. Ibid., 120.

146. *Wichita Beacon*, October 4, 1912.

147. P.C. Day, "Notes on the Severe Heat & Drought over the Middle West during the Summer of 1913," *Monthly Weather Review* 41, 1433–56. Climatological Service, Illinois Section, Springfield. Washington, D.C.: USGPO, 1913.

148. Simpson, "Brief History of Emerson Carey's Carey Salt Company," 100.

149. Ibid., 121.

150. Welsh, *Hutchinson*, 129.

151. *Hutchinson News*, March 23, 2008.

152. Dorce Stapleton, interview with author, June 23, 2018.

153. Simpson, "Brief History of Emerson Carey's Carey Salt Company," 100.

154. *Senate Journal*, 3, 821–22.

155. Simpson, "Brief History of Emerson Carey's Carey Salt Company," 123.

156. Isely, *Arkansas Valley Interurban*, 13, 64–65.

157. Schulz, "Albright Airfield."

158. *Topeka Kansas News*, September 11, 1921.

159. *Industrial Refrigeration, Ice and Refrigeration Journal*, January 1916, 9.

160. Welsh, *Hutchinson*, 46.

161. Ploughe, *History of Reno County*, 160.

162. *Hutchinson News*, October 6, 1916.

Chapter 7

163. This section regarding Emerson's role as fuel administrator is based on Simpson, "Brief History of Emerson Carey's Carey Salt Company," 120; General Orders of the United States Fuel Administration, 33; *Topeka Daily Capital Journal*, January 31, 1918.

164. *Topeka Daily Capital*, December 13, 1917.

165. General Orders of the United States Fuel Administration, 33; *Topeka Daily Capital Journal*, January 30, 1918; *Fort Scott Daily*, January 31, 1918. Harry Garfield was the federal fuel administrator under whom Emerson served as local administrator during World War I. Because of Garfield's obligations to curtail coal usage, he was not a popular figure during a time of harsh winter and general coal shortages. Local newspapers compared Emerson to Garfield for the same reasons.

166. *Lawrence Daily Journal World*, January 1, 1918.

167. *Fort Scott Daily Tribune/Fort Scott Daily Monitor*, March 19, 1918.

168. *Hutchinson News*, September 19, 1918.

169. Shortage of Coal: Hearings.

170. Carey Salt Scrapbooks, copy of letter sent from United States fuel administrator Harry Garfield in Washington, D.C., during World War I, December 20, 1918.

171. Ploughe, *History of Reno County*, 33–36.
172. Simpson, "Brief History of Emerson Carey's Carey Salt Company," 99.
173. Ibid., 160–62.
174. Ibid., 100.
175. *Park and Cemetery and Landscape Gardening*, 88, 89.
176. Cemetery Records of Reno County, 374; Crystal Braxton, interview with author, July 9, 2018.
177. Sharon Kidwell, *Sunflower Quarterly* 9, no. 2 (August 1987): 16, 17.
178. Carey, "Autobiography of Emerson Carey," 28.
179. *Hutchinson News*, May 31, 1919.
180. American Automobiles, "The Marmon Automobile," www.american-automobiles.com/Marmon-1916-1925.html.
181. *Hutchinson News*, May 17, 1919.
182. *Topeka State Journal*, "Bare Blackmail Plot," June 14, 1919, 2.
183. *Wichita Daily Eagle*, January 3, 1920, 10.
184. "Inflation Calculator," U.S. Official Inflation Data, Alioth Finance, July 9, 2018, www.officialdata.org.
185. *Industrial Refrigeration, Ice and Refrigeration Journal*, various issues between 1904 and 1919.
186. This section regarding the Egg Case Filler Corporation is based on Simpson, "Brief History of Emerson Carey's Carey Salt Company," 89; *Hutchinson News*, December 13, 1918.
187. *American Lumberman*, "New Western Wall Board Manufacturer," 90, December 4, 1920.
188. *Park and Cemetery and Landscape Gardening*, 88, 89.
189. Author's recollection.
190. *Hutchinson News*, May 7, 1919.
191. Simpson, "Brief History of Emerson Carey's Carey Salt Company," 111.
192. *Public Service Magazine*, 181.
193. *Hutchinson News*, May 17, 1919.
194. Simpson, "Brief History of Emerson Carey's Carey Salt Company," 114.
195. Ibid.; *Hutchinson Gazette*, March 1924.
196. *Hutchinson News*, July 17, 1920.
197. Simpson, "Brief History of Emerson Carey's Carey Salt Company," 114.
198. *Hutchinson News*, July 9, 1921.

199. *Hutchinson Daily News*, December 6, 1922.
200. *Hutchinson News*, April 1, 1920.
201. *So-we-kan*, 19.
202. Ibid.; Simpson, "Brief History of Emerson Carey's Carey Salt Company," 98.
203. Simpson, "Brief History of Emerson Carey's Carey Salt Company," 98; "Inflation Calculator."
204. Simpson, "Brief History of Emerson Carey's Carey Salt Company," 124.

Chapter 8

205. *Hutchinson Daily News*, July 10, 1908.
206. Steve Conard and Steve Harmon, interview with author, June 12, 2018.
207. Boyd, "History of the City of Willowbrook"; *Topeka Kansas News*, September 11, 1921.
208. *Topeka State Journal*, July 1, 1922, 8, by "AJC"; *Wichita Sunday Eagle*, December 11, 1921.
209. Macdonald, *Prairie Dunes*, 9.
210. Boyd, "History of the City of Willowbrook"; *Topeka State Journal*, July 1, 1922, 8, by "AJC."
211. Welsh, *Hutchinson*, 210.
212. *Hutchinson News*, January 6, 1921.
213. Welsh, *Hutchinson*, 1946, 110.
214. Simpson, "Brief History of Emerson Carey's Carey Salt Company," 98.
215. Ibid., 84.

Chapter 9

216. Boyd, "History of the City of Willowbrook."
217. Macdonald, *Prairie Dunes*, 9.
218. *Hutchinson News*, July 5, 1923.
219. Simpson, "Brief History of Emerson Carey's Carey Salt Company," 148.
220. Ibid.; Ulrich, *Carey Salt Mine*, 13.
221. *Hutchinson News*, June 23, 1923; author's recollection.

222. Simpson, "Brief History of Emerson Carey's Carey Salt Company," 148.

223. Ibid., 160–62.

224. *Hutchinson Herald*, December 12, 1924.

225. *Hutchinson News*, January 20, 1923.

226. *Kansas: The First Century*, 25; Welsh, *Hutchinson*, 46; Simpson, "Brief History of Emerson Carey's Carey Salt Company," 98.

227. *Hutchinson News*, February 26, 1924.

228. *Hutchinson Gazette*, March 1924.

229. Carey interview, July 10, 2018.

230. *Hutchinson Daily News*, November 12, 1924.

231. *Hutchinson News*, November 15, 1924.

232. *Hutchinson News*, September 27, 1987.

233. *Kansas: The First Century*, 25.

234. Simpson, "Brief History of Emerson Carey's Carey Salt Company," 85; Sharon Kidwell, *Sunflower Quarterly* 9, no. 2 (August 1987): 16, 17.

235. *Hutchinson News*, March 23, 1926.

236. *Hutchinson News*, August 6 and August 15, 1925.

237. Simpson, "Brief History of Emerson Carey's Carey Salt Company," 160–62.

238. Boyd, "History of the City of Willowbrook," ch. III.

239. Dal Liddle, *Hutchinson News*, September 27, 1987.

240. *Hutchinson News*, April 22, 1927.

241. *Hutchinson News*, June 23 and September 10, 1928.

242. *Council Grove Republican*, May 9, 1927.

243. *Hutchinson News*, July 13, 1929.

244. ArchiveGrid, "Special Collections Carey Salt Company records, 1927–33, 1939 (bulk 1930–33)," Louisiana State University, beta.worldcat.org/archivegrid/data/268954252.

245. This section is based on Simpson, "Brief History of Emerson Carey's Carey Salt Company," 153–56; author's recollection.

246. Baker, "Reno County Court Houses," 7–11; Mitchell, *The Fair City*, postcard 41.

247. Welsh, *Hutchinson*, 110; "Inflation Calculator."

248. This section about Albright Field is based on *Hutchinson News*, March 16, 23 and August 24, 1929; Schulz, "Albright Airfield."

249. Simpson, "Brief History of Emerson Carey's Carey Salt Company," 160–62.

250. Boyd, "History of the City of Willowbrook," ch. III.

251. Simpson, "Brief History of Emerson Carey's Carey Salt Company," 153–56.
252. *Hutchinson News*, July 26, 1930.
253. *Hutchinson Herald*, May 24, 1931.
254. Simpson, "Brief History of Emerson Carey's Carey Salt Company," 91.

Chapter 10

255. *Kansas, The First Century*, 25; Welsh, *Hutchinson*, 127.
256. Carey interview, July 10, 2018; More About Laparoscopic Colectomy.
257. Simpson, "Brief History of Emerson Carey's Carey Salt Company," 91.
258. Ibid., 99.
259. Ibid., 85.
260. The paragraphs in this chapter about the construction of the Emerson Carey memorial and the subsequent ceremony are based on various newspaper articles from *Hutchinson News* in 1934 and 1935: February 13, 1934; March 23, 1934; August 14, 1934; September 10, 1934; July 2, 1935; August 21, 1935; October 2, 1935; October 24, 1935; October 25, 1935.

BIBLIOGRAPHY

Books

Connelley, William E. *A Standard History of Kansas and Kansans.* Vol. 5. Chicago: Lewis, 1918.

De La Praudiere, Edelin, ed. *Historical References of the City of Hutchinson, Kansas.* Hutchinson, KS: Midwest Publishing and Distributing Co., 1931.
———. *Hutchinson: The Salt City.* Hutchinson, KS: Hutchinson Printing Company, 1910.

Hutchinson: The Salt City in the Heart of the Great Kansas Wheat Belt. Hutchinson, KS: Commercial Club, 1910.

Ice and Refrigeration Illustrated. Chicago: Nickerson & Collins Company, July 1904.

Isely, M.D. "Doc." *Arkansas Valley Interurban.* Glendale, CA: Mac Sebree, 1977.

Kansas: The First Century. Vol. 3. New York: Lewis Historical Publishing Company, 1956.

Macdonald, Peter, ed. *Prairie Dunes: The First Fifty Years, 1937–1987.* Newton, KS: Mennonite Press, 1987.

Mitchell, Pat. *The Fair City.* Topeka, KS: Jostens Printing and Publishing Division, 1986.

Moody's Manual of Railroads and Corporation Securities. Vol. 12, 1848. New York: Moody Manual Company, 1911.

National Cyclopaedia of American Biography. New York: James T. White and Co., 1948.

Ploughe, Sheridan. *History of Reno County, Kansas: Its People, Industries, and Institutions.* Vol. 2. Indianapolis, IN: Bowen & Company, Inc., 1917.

Sheehan, Leo, ed. *The Salt City Industrial Review and Commercial Booklet of Hutchinson.* Hutchinson, KS: News Company Printers, 1910.

Ulrich, Barbara C. *The Carey Salt Mine.* Charleston, SC: Arcadia Publishing, 2008.

Welsh, Willard. *Hutchinson, A Prairie City in Kansas.* N.p., 1946

Other Materials

Baker, Mary Lynn. "Reno County Court Houses." *Legacy, the Journal of the Reno County Historical Society* 2, no. 2 (1990): 7–11.

Boyd, Bob. "A History of the City of Willowbrook." Paper, College English II, Emporia State University, 1964.

Carey, Emerson. "Autobiography of Emerson Carey." Located at the Reno County Museum, Hutchinson, KS.

Carey, Patty. "Emerson Carey, and His Industrial Empire." Paper, located at the Reno County Museum, Hutchinson, KS.

Carey Salt Scrapbooks. Located at the Reno County Museum. Hutchinson, KS.

Cemetery Records of Reno County Kansas: 1865–1978. North Newton, KS: Reno County Genealogical Society, Mennonite Press, 1980.

Fred Henny Scrapbook of Hutchinson newspaper articles, Hutchinson Public Library.

General Orders, Regulations and Rulings of the United States Fuel Administration, August 10, 1917–December 31, 1918. Harvard Law Library, Gift of the United States Fuel Administration. Washington, D.C.: General Printing Office, 1919.

Green's Hutchinson Directory. Hutchinson, KS, 1888.

Hanes, J.E., comp., former manager, Morton Salt Company. "The History of the Salt Industry in Grand Saline." archive.lib.msu.edu/DMC/sliker/ msuspcsbs_mort_mortonsalt15/msuspcsbs_mort_mortonsalt15.pdf. Revised by R.F. Hardiman, manager, December 17, 1945 (accessed May 30, 2018).

Hutchinson City Directory. Des Moines, IA: Herbert & Early, 1897.

Kidwell, Sharon. "Fairlawn Burial Park." *Sunflower Quarterly* (Reno County Genealogical Society Newsletter) 9, no. 2 (August 1987): 16, 17.

The National Provisioner 40 (March 6, 1909).

Pacific Reporter. St. Paul, MN: West Publishing Company, n.d.

Park and Cemetery and Landscape Gardening. Vols. 28–30. Chicago: Allied Arts Publishing Company, 1920.

Plat Book of Reno County. Minneapolis, MN: Northwest Publishing Company, 1902.

Pocket City Directory. Hutchinson, KS: Roberts-Payne Printing Company, 1900.

Public Service Magazine. Vols. 32–33. 1922

Reno County Museum artifact collection.

Schulz, Philip. "Albright Airfield—Hutchinson's First Airport." *Legacy, the Journal of the Reno County Historical Society*. Hutchinson, KS, 2013

Senate Journal, Proceedings of the Senate of the United State of Kansas, Nineteenth Biennial Session, Topeka, January 12 to March 24, 1915. Burt E. Brown, Secretary. Topeka: Kansas State Printing Office, 1915.

Shortage of Coal: Hearings…65th Congress, 2nd Session, Pursuant to Senate Resolution 163, a Resolution Directing the Committee on Manufactures to Investigate the Causes of the Shortage of Coal and Sugar. United States Federal Trade Commission, United States Congress, Senate. Committee on Manufactures. Washington, D.C.: U.S. Government Printing Office, 1918.

Simpson, George W. July. "A Brief History of Emerson Carey's Carey Salt Company, 1901–1956." Master's thesis, Kansas State Teachers College. Emporia, KS, 1956.

So-we-kan: Southwestern Kansas. Hutchinson, KS: Hutchinson Gazette, 1920.

Stewart, Harry. "It Pays to Hang On: The Life Story of Emerson Carey." *American Magazine*, 1925.

Websites

American Automobiles. www.american-automobiles.com.

Digital Sterling. "History of Sterling." Sterling.digitalsckls.info/history-of-sterling.

Find a Grave. www.findagrave.com.

Hubco Inc. www.Hubcoinc.com.

Kansas Historical Society. www.Kshs.org.

More About Laparoscopic Colectomy. www.Lapsurgery.com/history.htm.

Wikipedia. www.wikipedia.org.

INDEX

U

Underwood Packing Company 31
United States Packing Company 64

V

Valley State Bank 28
Vincent, Frank 41, 63

W

wages 15, 18
Western Ice Manufacturers 51, 56
Western Strawboard Company 58
Western Straw Products Company
      59, 76
Whiteside, Houston 35, 60
White Steamer 58
Williams, Charles M. 46, 52, 54, 89,
      121, 132
Willowbrook 101, 105, 114, 118, 121
Winchester, Charles S. 34, 45
Winchester Packing Company 34,
      49, 87
Winton 64

ABOUT THE AUTHORS

Lynn Ledeboer has worked for the Reno County Historical Society (the parent company that owns both Strataca-Kansas Underground Salt Museum and the Reno County Museum) for eleven years. In that time, she became a bit obsessed with all things salty, so having the opportunity to write about Emerson Carey, one of the most illustrious salt magnates in the area, was a perfectly logical extension of that passion. As curator of the museums, Lynn enjoys all of the many artifacts and stories that bring Reno County history to life. Before entering the museum world, Lynn dabbled in many far-reaching world experiences, from painting outhouses, to performing psychological testing, to working as a microbiology laboratory technician for a company that made pizza toppings.

Myron Marcotte's obsession with all things Carey began in a fifth-grade class when he saw a film about the Carey Salt Mine and the Carey offices. He became intrigued with the idea of becoming a salt miner. In 1975, that intrigue turned to reality when he began working at the mine. After thirty-seven years of working underground, he rose to the level of mine manager. Along the way, he appeared in and was a consultant for three television series: *Dirty Jobs* salt mine episode; *How Stuff Works*: "Salt"; and *Modern Marvel*: "Secrets Underground." In the back of his mind, he had always admired Emerson Carey and his accomplishments in Hutchinson. He retired from mining in 2013 and immediately went to work for the Reno County Historical Society at Strataca-Kansas Underground Salt Museum as a mine specialist. He never really left the mine—just moved next door. You can learn more about Myron by visiting his IMDB page at www.imdb.com/name/nm4836611.